POCKET GUIDE TO
Knots & Splices

POCKET GUIDE TO
Knots & Splices

DES PAWSON

CHARTWELL
BOOKS, INC.

Contents

This edition published in 2002 by
CHARTWELL BOOKS, INC.
A division of BOOK SALES, INC
114 Northfield Avenue,
Edison, New Jersey 08837

Produced by
PRC Publishing Ltd,
64 Brewery Road,
London N7 9NT

A member of **Chrysalis** Books plc

ISBN 0 7858 1446 9

Printed and bound in China

ACKNOWLEDGMENTS
The publisher wishes to thank Simon Clay for taking
all the photography in this book, with the following
exceptions:

© Earl & Nazima Kowall/CORBIS for page 7 (top
    right);
© Bettmann/CORBIS for page 7 (top left);
© Gianni Dagli Orti/CORBIS for page 7 (bottom);
    The photograph on page 8 (bottom right) is
    reproduced by permission of the British Library
    (Ms number: Cott. Nero. D. IV; Folio: 211);
© James L Amos/CORBIS for page 12
    (bottom right).
Many thanks to Marlow Ropes of Hailsham, UK, for
    their help in supplying the photograph on page 8
    (top right), and the exotic ropes on page 19.

Pocket Guide to Knots & Splices

Preface

We all use knots but do you use them properly? There are many knots to choose from and this book will give you the choice you need to do a proper job. Please start with some of the more simple knots, before going on to the more complex knots. There is a great logic to most of the knots we use and careful attention to both the photographs, the arrows in the photographs and the text should give you the ability to tie all these  knots. Do not expect to remember every knot from the first time you tie it, this pocket book is here to remind you. The more you use a knot the easier it will become. The art of tying good and proper knots is well worth striving for.

May my book help you.

Good luck.
Des Pawson
Ipswich. 2001

Introduction

Knots have been with us since the beginning of time. They are not just restricted to mankind. Gorillas tie creepers together to make their nests. Birds make nests with a knotted weave. The hag fish [eptatretus stoutii], found on the eastern shores of the Pacific, ties itself in a knot as protection. There are even knots to be found in DNA. This is without thinking of the accidental formation of knots in creepers and other plants.

As man first evolved he, too, would have taken the creepers, grasses, animal skins, and sinews that came to hand and used them as primitive cordage with which to tie knots. Unfortunately these organic materials decay, and need very special, extreme circumstances to survive, leaving very little evidence for us today. Yet by circumstantial evidence we know that earliest man, be he hunter or herder, had material with which he would tie knots. Some prehistoric beads and pendants with perforations to take some kind of cord were found in caves in Austria. These items were dated about 300,000 years old, and if a cord went through the holes it would have to be joined . . . with a knot! From 100,000

years ago there is evidence of man cutting thongs, and in China objects have been identified as needles, implying that sewing and knotting took place. Some 80,000-year-old spear points have been found that had to be lashed to poles; 40,000 years ago part of mankind was living in tent-like structures, which suggests some knotting taking place. Burials at Sungir´ in Russia, 25,000 years ago, have produced a wide range of beads and perforated fox teeth that it is thought were sewn to clothing. There is some evidence that European cave dwellers who decorated their caves with paintings used some form of scaffolding that would have needed plenty of knots and lashings to build. A small fragment of fossilized two-ply cord has been found in the Lascaux caves in France.

As mankind migrated across the world, people would have crossed substantial stretches of water. To achieve this some form of flotation aid or boat would have been needed, which in itself would be likely to require knots and lashings. This crossing of the waters goes back at least 700,000 years, with many crossings to what is now Australia taking place about 30,000 years ago, yet the

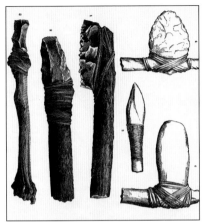

Above Left: Stone Age tools with lashings.

Above: Rope bridges require sophisticated rope and knot work.

Left: Early 17th century representation of the Inca Quipus.

7

Above: Example of Chinese knotting.

Above Right: 2,000-year-old rope made from papyrus reeds, used to transport 68-ton blocks of stone.

Right: The Celts created wonderful inter-weaves. This example is from the famous *Lindisfarne Gospels*.

oldest known boat, found in a peat bog in Denmark is a mere 8,000 years old.

The first actual knot to be found is the sheet bend, used to make up a fishing net, complete with weights and floats, found on the Karelian Isthmus, between Russia and Finland. The actual knot is 9,000 years old, yet we still use exactly the sheet bend for the same purpose today.

A number of archaeological finds in Danish peat bogs, dating between 8,000 and 3,500 years old, have preserved examples of cords and bindings. Other interesting finds have been made in association with Swiss lakeside dwellings going back 4,500 years.

It was the ice that helped preserve another interesting example of cordage, found on the 5,300-year-old "Ice man" recently discovered buried in a glacier between Switzerland and Italy. He was carrying cordage made of lime bast, and some net, perhaps for catching birds. He also had a knife or dagger that consisted of a piece of flint lashed tightly to a wooden handle, and the handle was fitted with a lanyard so that the knife would not be lost if dropped, which is still good practice today.

From as long ago as 4,500 years ago we find good evidence of knots in the Pyramids and tombs of the pharaohs in Egypt. The actual pyramids needed ropes of considerable strength to move the huge blocks of stone from which they were built. On the door to one of the tombs was a piece of rope that looked as if it had been made yesterday—a perfect piece of three-strand Z-laid (see page 16) rope about half an inch in diameter. On the wall in another burial chamber was found a painting, dated 3,500 years old, of men making rope in a manner still used by some of the local people today. Inside another tomb a model ship was found with the planks lashed together rather than nailed. Here are many examples of knots, splices, and other sophisticated ropework showing that these people really knew how to use rope and knots.

Later, when Xerxes crossed with his army from Asia to Europe in 492BC, he employed Phoenician and Egyptian rope makers to supply the ropes that held together two bridges of boats. It has been worked out from Herodotus's account of this amazing feat that the rope could well have been eight or nine inches in diameter, very competent ropemaking by any account, and nearly 2,500 years ago.

Throughout time each civilization and cultural group has made its own contribution to the world of knots. The Chinese developed a series of very complex decorative knots together with whole layers of meaning, both in the knots and in the colors of the cord in which those knots are tied.

The Celtic cultures gave rise to wonderful intricate interweaves, developed from the modest braids, interwoven knots such as the carrick bend, and what we today call the Turk's head. These simple knot designs, which can be found all over the world, were extended and stretched into the fantastic borders, panels, and other decorative motives found carved on wood and stone, and used as decoration in those highly decorated bibles and gospels such as the Lindisfarne Gospels, the Book of Kells, and the Book of Durrow.

It was the knotted fringes of Arabia spreading to Europe via Italy and Spain that gave rise to macrame. This almost lace-like collection of simple knots has had many periods of popularity, especially in the very late nineteenth and early twentieth centuries, with a major revival in the 1970s. Sailors also enjoyed this work calling it "square knotting," or "McNamara's lace" when worked as a fringe to canvas.

As soon as man ventured onto the sea rope and knots must have been at work, and as seafarers ranged further and

further so their ships became more sophisticated and their use of rope and knots developed. One only has to look at the lashings on a Pacific sea-going canoe to realize just how well man can use knots and lashings. But the seagoing peoples of the Pacific also used knots in another way, they used knotted cords as an aid to memory in their navigation.

The Incas of the Andes developed a very intricate method of communicating using knotted strings. These were known as Quipus, and with them very sophisticated records and accounts could be kept, without written records. The Inca civilization was destroyed in the middle of the sixteenth century and we are left with only a few examples of the actual Quipus, a few drawings from the time and very little else. Research is still being undertaken to establish the exact nature of how these items worked. It has been established that a variety of knots were used and the color of the strings and their relationship with one another were of significance. It is certain that, with the aid of these collections of knots and strings, the very complex tasks of taxing, governing, and organizing the distribution of goods over a large area could be carried out to a very detailed level.

Above: Sailor's wall pocket with McNamara's lace.

Left: Early 20th century macrame bag.

This use of knots for communication was taken up again much later in the late nineteenth century by David Macheath and Robert Mylne in Scotland when an alphabet for the blind was developed. It did not come to anything, but was part of an on-going tradition of knots for communication. The knot tied in a hand-kerchief to remind you of a task to be

Right: The business
end of a lariat and
examples of
cowboy's rawhide
braiding.

Below: A selection of
ropework fenders.

Below Right: A detail
of ship's standing
rigging—note the
double wall knot (see
page 59).

performed is but a simple manifestation of this principle. Many cultures place significance in the tying and untying of knots. For example, the name Canute [knot] expressed the hope that the child so named was the mother's last. Some special occasions—such as weddings—include the symbolic untying of a series of knots as a countdown to the event itself. There are records of witches who sold knots to be untied by sailors to release the wind. Other knots were said to bring good luck, while there were others that brought bad luck. It was said that some knots could inflict disease or illness yet other knots cured. The knot we know as the reef or square knot was called the Hercules knot by the ancient Greeks and Romans, as they believed that the god himself had invented it. They thought that it had many magic powers, including the ability to heal wounds quickly. It is still the best knot to tie together the end of a bandage or sling because it lies square or flat, or perhaps because it has a little magic?

Knots and love also go together. It is still said to this day that to get married is to "tie the knot"—the marriage knot is a knot tied with the mouth that cannot be untied with the teeth. There are a number of knots that have the name "true lovers knot." The one shown on page 236 is a good example, the two halves joined but also separate.

Every trade that has some cause to use rope, cords, or even threads needs knots and will have developed special knots peculiar to its own requirements, evolving the best solution to the environment and knotting problems. The surgeon has his special knot tied with forceps; the weaver a number of special knots evolved with speed of tying in mind. Anglers and fishermen have developed many special knots for their fishing hooks, and often have their own peculiar ways of joining lines and making up their nets. Farmers and cowboys have evolved special halters, hobbles, and lariat knots, with cowboys making the most intricately braided horse gear using rawhide. The making of whips developed into a wonderful art practiced both by horsemen themselves as well as tradesmen making the most intricate braided items to be sold through the tack shop. The wagoner's hitch is still to be seen today, used by truckers to tie down loads and covers just as it was in the days of old on a horse-drawn wagon.

It is at sea, in ships, that man was most intimately dependent on rope and the skill to use it.

"To put a marlinespike in a man's hand and to set him to work on a piece of rigging is considered a fair trial of his qualities as an able seaman."

So wrote R. H. Dana in 1845 in *The Seaman's Friend* and he went on,

"The rigging of a ship requires constant mending, covering and working upon in a multitude of ways."

The basic rigging of a ship would be done before she set sail by shore-based riggers, but as soon as she had started her voyage, work began setting the rigging to the master's own special ideas. The master of a sailing ship took great pride in the appearance of the ship yet kept a close eye on the costs, and would use the free labor of the most skilled ropeworker to add details of decorative ropework to the ship herself, with manropes, decorative strops on some of the blocks, coach-whipped rails, and fancy mats. The ship's bell deserved a display of those fancy knots that told the world what degree of skill was available on the ship. The smart appearance of the master's own shore-going boat would be enhanced with, perhaps, decorative tiller lines, and superior decorative rope fenders. All these showed the world that the captain was master of a ship manned by the most skilled of seamen. It must not be thought that all this decorative rope work was only for show. Most decoration had a function as well, for example the footropes, those ropes hanging below the yards on which the sailor stood to furl the sails, would have Turk's head knots tied on them to stop the sailors' feet slipping.

It could be said that a sailor would be judged by the quality of the ropework with which he surrounded himself, such as on his sea-chest with the handles or beckets, well-made grommets parcelled, wormed, leathered, and finished with Turk's heads, or a far more demanding pair of hitched, grafted, and coach-whipped chest beckets. The lanyard or handle to his seabag, or the non-slip handle on his knife, all showed the owner's skill with rope, speaking far clearer than any certificate of his ability to understand and use the appropriate ropework for any task. This ropework would also tell of his ability to stick to a job over a long period of time, for a pair of fancy chest beckets could easily take up forty or fifty hours snatched from dog watches, Sundays in the tropics, and other odd moments of spare time that could be contrived and sleep that could be given up; perhaps the fruits of one or even two voyages. Men would trade knots among themselves, vying with one another to produce the best work, encouraging the beginners to show that they were real sailors.

He could prepare for the next run ashore by making himself a life preserver, walking stick, or night stick, or perhaps a knotted rope animal, a bag, or mat as a gift .The rope mat at the entry of the home would signify the fact that this was the home of a man who worked at sea. The sailor, often part of an international crew and so in contact with knots from around the world, was an ambassador for and collector of knots, spreading and trading knot knowledge around the globe.

To give some idea as to just how much skill and knowledge these ropeworking artists could possess, C. W. Ashley in his monumental work, *The Ashley Book of Knots* (1944), illustrates over 3,500 differing knots, splices, and other ropeworking techniques. Far less rope is used at sea today, yet it is still true to say that a ship cannot go to sea without ropes and there can be found some very special examples of ropework in hi tech fibers on the rigging of today's racing yacht. There is still the occasional sailor who will spend his spare time

creating beautiful examples of ropework rather than watching a video, carrying on the tradition of the old time sailor.

It is not just the oldest methods of transport that need knots, the world of space travel found that knots tying together bundles of cables performed better than clips—so, remember those knots circling the sky in our communication satellites. There will be a need for knots on the moon, just as we still need knots today in all walks of life.

Above: Examples of sailors' decorative ropework.

Equipment

Over the centuries mankind has made rope from many materials, both plant fibers and animal fibers. These may be twisted or plaited together. In the past this would have been done by hand or with very primitive machines. Today, many new synthetic materials have been developed, far stronger than the natural fibers, and machines have been built that can make thousands of feet of rope in a day.

Twisted rope is made by twisting (or spinning) together fibers in one direction to make yarn, then a number of yarns are twisted (or to use the rope-making term "**laid up**") together in the opposite direction to make a strand. Three or four of these strands are then usually laid together with an opposite twist to make the rope. Occasionally three ropes may be twisted together again in the opposite direction to make what is called "cable laid rope," usually referred to as "cable."

There can be much confusion as to the description of the direction of the twist of any one of the components. The industry standard is to define it by the letters S and Z, the body of the appropriate letter signifying the direction of the twist as seen in the yarn, strand, or rope. This avoids the question as to what is meant by left and right, which could refer to the direction shown in the twist or the direction in which the twist is applied.

Much of the rope used today, especially that using fiber from synthetic materials, is braided. Sometimes it is braided as a hollow tube, sometimes with a core which may consist of yarns of the same or different material braided, twisted, or left parallel. There are also braids made from eight or twelve heavy strands, half the strands being S-laid and the other Z. This gives a rope that does not easily kink and makes an ideal anchor rope.

Cordage is the collective word for all types and sizes of rope, and there is a great choice of fibers that cordage can be made from. Each of the fibers has its own properties and may be just right for a certain job. There are two main groups of fibers: those made from natural materials derived directly from plants and synthetic or man-made fibers that are chemically created, being extruded from machines as continuous fibers.

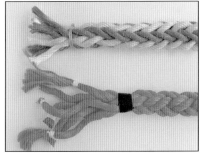

Above: Braided rope with braided core (left), Hollow braid rope (center), and Braided rope with a twisted core (right).

Above Left: Z (left) and S-laid rope (right).

Center Left: Twelve-plait rope (top) and Eight or square-plait rope (bottom).

Below Left: A cable consisting of three ropes of three strands, each strand made from yarns and fibers.

Hemp is a natural fiber obtained from the stem of the plant *Cannabis sativa*. It has been used to make cordage of all sorts for hundreds of years. Hemp makes one of the strongest natural-fiber ropes, but it does have a tendency to rot if left wet for a long period of time, so in the past it was frequently tarred. This slightly reduced its strength but greatly extended its life. Supplies of rope made from this material are rare today.

Manila is a fiber obtained from the wild banana plant, *Musa textilis*, and was introduced from the Philippines at the beginning of the nineteenth century. The word "hemp" had become synonymous with rope fiber and the place of origin was used to describe the quality—for example, St. Petersburg hemp, Riga hemp, Italian hemp—all from the cannabis plant. When this new rope fiber was introduced from the Philippines it was called "Manila hemp," giving rise to some confusion. This ropemaking material proved to be as strong as real hemp and was more resistant to rot, so rarely needed to be tarred. Manila rope is still being made, and exported from the Philippines today, although sadly the quality is not what it was 70 or more years ago.

Sisal is a rope-making fiber derived from *Agave sisalana*, a cactus-type plant from Central America. It is weaker than Manila or hemp and requires treating with chemicals to make it waterproof and rot-resistant. First exported from a port on the Yucatan peninsula that sounded like Sisal, it is now grown in many parts of the world as a low-cost cordage fiber used to make rope, small twines, and string.

Coir is derived from the outer part of the coconut. It has been used as cordage for centuries in the Indian sub-continent. It is not very strong but is light, so large ropes or cables can be made. In fact, it is the only natural rope that will float. It is fairly resistant to rot in salt water. When made up into a rope it has a high degree of stretch, so was used in the past as tow ropes and even mooring ropes as the stretch reduced the strain put upon the ship as it jerked about. When used in the West, rope made from Coir was sometimes referred to as "Bass" or "Grass" rope.

Cotton is also used for making cordage, mainly small ropes and twines, and, because it can be spun so finely, it is especially good for making

Top Left: Natural-fiber ropes. From left to right: hemp; tarred hemp; Manila; sisal; coir; cotton.

Center Left: Exotics. From left to right: Kevlar over a Vectran core; Kevlar core; Dynema with a Spectra core; Vectran core; PBO.

Bottom Left: Synthetic fiber ropes. From left to right: fibrillated; split-film; staplespun; multifilament; polypropylene; terylene; nylon.

small braided cords. It was rarely used at sea except for fishing nets. As cotton is prone to rot, the fishing nets needed frequent dipping in some form of preservative, such as the tannin derived from barks of various trees, tar, or chemicals like copper sulphate or c opper naphthenate.

Nylon was the first synthetic material that was suitable for making rope. Developed in the mid-1930s, at first it was very expensive and also very stretchy. Slowly the scientists were able to reduce both its cost of production and the degree of stretch. Today's nylon rope is very strong, more than two and a half times the strength of hemp. It still has some stretch in it, but this makes it especially good for use where there may be sudden shock loads applied, such as mooring ropes, tow ropes, and climbing ropes. As a heavy monofilament yarn, nylon is also used for most fishing line. Nylon ropes lose about 5–10% of their strength when wet. Nylon rope wears very well, it is resistant to chafe and to mildew and rot.

Polyester, also known as Dacron or Terylene, was developed in the 1940s.

It is fractionally weaker than nylon and holds its strength when wet. It resists rot and chafe. It is the material of choice for many yacht ropes as it has little stretch, and can even be bought as special prestretched ropes that have even lower stretch.

Polypropylene was developed in the 1950s. Though not as strong as nylon and polyester, it is considerably cheaper. It was the availability of low-cost rope made from polypropylene that really marginalized the production of natural-fiber rope. Polypropylene is light in weight so it will float, making it useful for rescue ropes and short mooring ropes. It must be noted, however, that polypropylene does not resist abrasion well and, even though today's polypropylenes are treated with ultraviolet light inhibitors, UV rays still cause the rope to break down far quicker than polyester or nylon. To counter the natural stiffness and slipperiness of the straight polypropylene yarn, it is processed and produced in a number of forms. Monofilament polypropylene rope is the most resistant to chafe. Multifilament is much softer and easier to knot and handle. Staplespun, where the fibers have been chopped up and then spun, giving a hairy rope, has much more grip. Splitfilm rope is the most inexpensive of all the polypropylenes, some ropes being only fit for one-off, temporary, or disposable tasks. Some manufacturers have developed a brown fibrillated version of the polypropylene fiber that looks very similar to hemp and has been used on some traditional boats for that old-time look. Recently a number of manufacturers have started mixing the polypropylene material with polyester or polyethylene at the extrusion stage of fiber production, to make various copolymer ropes that have a much greater strength and chafe resistance, yet are not much more expensive than the better quality polypropylenes

Exotic rope materials have been developed over the last few years that are lighter, stronger and have less stretch than anything seen so far. They are being used to replace wire rope rigging on racing yachts, and in various hi-tech industrial uses. All these exotics are sold under various trade names or initials to represent the complicated chemicals from which they are constructed. In order of their appear-ance on the market they are: Kevlar/Twaron/Technora (aramid), Spectra/Dynema (HMP, high modu-lous polyethelenes), Vectran (LCP, liquid crystal polymer), and Zylon (PBO, poly [P-phenylene-3, 6-benzo-bisoxazole]). In the main, they are not yet for everyday use, although HMP has started to be used in some fishing lines and kite lines. They are very expensive, and have various draw-backs such as their vulnerability to light or chafe, so are often covered with another material, usually polyester. Some of these materials do not work well on tight curves, which means that knots reduce their strength and so special splices or terminals have to be developed. One thing can be certain, that the scientist will continue to develop yet more and better rope mak-ing materials, and craftsmen will have to learn how best to use them.

Whatever the rope is made from, it is a valuable commodity and it needs looking after, Natural-fiber ropes need to be dried out properly if they get wet. All ropes need to be kept clean, as sand, salt, dirt, and oil working their way into a rope will wear it out from the inside. So, a good wash and scrub will extend the life of a rope, using some detergent if it is available. Coil and hang rope up to dry out after washing. Even though synthetic rope will not rot, it is better that it is stored dry.

Some people find that rope has a mind of its own and likes nothing better that to get into a complete tangle. Much of this is due to the way that rope is coiled and uncoiled, because when doing this a degree of twist is imparted to the rope. It is, therefore, important to coil and uncoil the rope in the appropriate manner to keep this twist to a minimum. Always uncoil a new Z-laid rope in an anticlockwise direction. Likewise, whenever the rope is coiled up, do that in a clockwise direction. Of course, should you ever come across S-laid rope, deal with it in exactly the opposite manner. For braided rope, either use the special figure-of-eight method of coiling or the flake method. These coiling methods balance the twist in the rope. If for some reason you must make a plain circular coil with braided rope, make absolutely certain that when the coil is uncoiled it is done in the opposite way to which it was coiled. Whatever method you use, if you get kinks and twists in any rope,

run the rope through your hands several times to get out all the unwanted twists. If, when you are making a coil, the rope starts to build up a lot of twist, it will help to spin the whole coil held in your hand to get rid of the kinks as they start to develop.

Having made your coil, there are a number of ways to keep the coil tidily in its place, so that when the time comes, it is easily used. The coil can be tied up in three or four places with thin pieces of line or "stops." This is often how rope is delivered from the makers. The tail end of the rope may be used to self-stop the rope, giving a round coil. The buntline or gasket coil is another way of storing the rope in a tidy and accessible manner, this time in a "hank" form. Whether you use the self-stop coil or the buntline coil, if the tail end is used as a bight to make the stop, you will be left with a convenient loop from which to hang the coil. For illustrations of these techniques see pages 24–25.

There is an old seafarers' saying that goes something like, "every hair a rope yarn, every finger a marlinespike, their blood is Stockholm tar." The tar used for preserving the rope was used so much that a sailor would always

Above: Coiling Z-laid rope.

Below: The figure-of-eight method for coiling braided rope.

Making a Self Stopped Coil

1 Having made a plain coil fold the short end back on itself to make a bight and start to wrap round the whole of the coil trapping the bight under the turns.

2 Make several turns round the rope coil and tuck the remaining short end through the bight.

3 Push the turns tight up against the tucked end.

4 Finished coil

5 A self stopped coil. The turns made with the rope end doubled to give a hanging loop.

6 A coil of Z laid rope coiled correctly and held together with stoppings of fine line.

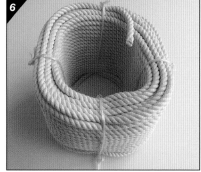

Making up a Bunline or Gasket Coil

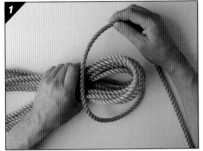

1   Make a plain coil and then hold it together at one end, making a hank with a hole at the end. Bring the short working part back and down to your hand.
2   Wrap round with a few turns.
3   Make bight in the working part
4   Bring the bight through the hole at the top of the hank.
5   Bring the bight down to the same level as the first round turns to complete the buntline coil.

smell of it, hence being referred to as a "tar" or "Jack tar." A marlinespike is a steel spike, anything from six to nearly twenty-four inches long, used to make splices, work knots tight, and undo knots. A similar tool, only a little fatter and made from some form of hardwood, is called a "fid" and is used in much the same way. Sometimes the fid would have been made from whalebone, while a farmer might use a cow horn. A steel spike with a wooden handle is called a "pricker."

The marlinespike most often found in a yacht chandlers today has a flattened handle with a slot in it for undoing shackles. Today, there is a tool known as a Swedish fid that has a wooden handle and a hollow steel blade, which allows a strand of rope to be passed through the hole formed by the blade. If you can get hold of one, the Swedish fid makes work considerably easier. A marlinespike can be made from a six-inch nail, a pricker from a screwdriver, and a fid carved from any suitable piece of hardwood. A knife and/or scissors are always needed to cut and trim rope. A pair of pliers can sometimes be of help to pull a short end tight. A piece of bent stiff wire, ideally piano wire, will make a

loop tool for pulling small strands through fancy knots.

There are occasions when a heavy needle is needed. Ideally this should be a sailmaker's needle, which has a triangular section to its end, making a hole slightly larger than the eye so that the twine will pull through with ease. These needles need something to push them through. The correct tool is called a sailmaker's palm, a kind of strap that fits over the hand with a metal plate built in to push the needle. One other useful tool is adhesive tape ideally in a dispenser of some type. This is useful in a temporary way to stop a rope end from coming unlaid, and can be formed into a point to assist tucking.

Old-time sailors would have personalized their tools with decorative knots and carvings, maybe fixed a lanyard to some of them so they would not get lost, and kept them in a canvas bag called a "ditty" bag. There is no reason why you should not do the same with the tools of today.

Above Right: Tools from the past.

Bottom Right: Modern tools.

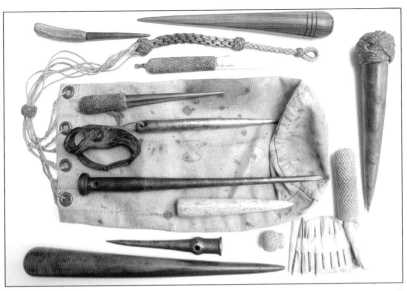

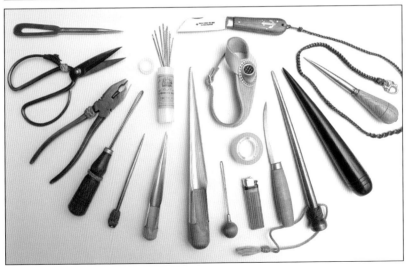

27

Basic Techniques

To tie a knot you need a piece of rope and the knowledge of how to tie the knot. This book contains that knowledge, but you will need to learn to get the most from the book. To help describe how to tie a knot, words have evolved over the years to describe the various parts of the rope and the moves and shapes the rope takes as we are making knots. Some of these are self-explanatory. The end that we are using to make the knot is called the **working end**, and the length behind it is the **working part**. The other part of the rope not being used is the **standing part** with the very end not being used called the **standing end.**

Folding the rope back on itself will give a **bight** in the middle of the rope, and making a loop with the rope crossing itself is a **crossing turn**, or sometimes a **half hitch**. Take the rope round an object and it is a **turn**, with two turns being a **round turn**.

It can help if you actually follow the instructions for a very simple knot, that you probably know already, such as the overhand knot (see page 38) or the reef knot (see page 98). This will illustrate many of the terms in use in a

familiar place and they will not be so difficult to cope with when you get to more complex knots. Certainly you should not try to tie the most complex of the knots at the end of the book without building yourself a base to work from. Do not try to run before you can walk, even though we are all tempted down that road.

When you come to make a knot you may not notice, but there are actually two distinct stages. First, you need to make all the moves that are described. Second, you need to tighten or dress the knot into the correct form with the strands positioned correctly, everything being neat tidy and tight. For most knots you will probably do this with you fingers and thumbs almost without thinking

It is possible to make all the right moves and then pull the wrong ends of the knot and have either a different knot or a complete disaster. The tying of the reef knot (see page 98) and the way to make it collapse into a slip knot is a good example of this at work—so look for the shape of the finished knot and make sure that you have what you want. Do take care that the working

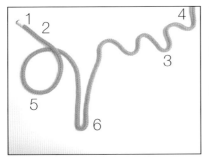

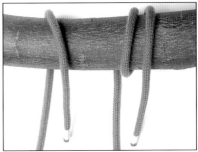

Above Left: Parts of a rope: 1 working end; 2 working part; 3 standing part; 4 standing end; 5 a crossing turn; 6 bight.

Above: Illustration of a turn (left) and round turn.

Left: The reef knot and (below) collapsed reef knot.

Below: The ends of the ropes are well defined in this photograph of a finished fisherman's knot (see page 116).

Above: Doubling is well illustrated in this stage of the figure-of-eight loop (see page 168).

Above: This stage in the Danish Kringle mat (see page 250) illustrates passing a bight.

Below: Dummying a knot—in this case a monkey's fist (see page 52).

Below: Working a knot tight with a spike.

end is not so short that it will pull out when the knot is put under strain. There is a useful type of knot called a slip knot that is designed as a quick release. It is undone or slipped very easily by pulling the short tail. It is essential that a slip knot is correctly tied, with the strain on the correct part, and that the loop and tail that form the quick-release part of the knot are jammed firmly in place. You should be certain it will stay that way until you decide you wish to release the knot.

Some knots are made in a single version and then the knot is doubled—for example, the figure-of-eight loop, water knot, and the mats and Turk's heads at the end of the book.

Very complex knots are often tied a little on the loose side and formed into the right shape before being tightened by working the slack out of the knot. You may find that a spike of some sort will help your fingers with this task. A spike is useful for tightening such knots as the monkey's fist (see page 52), man-rope knot (see page 64) or any of the Turk's heads (see pages 222 onward). Whatever the complex knot, when you come to tighten it you should do this systematically, working carefully from the beginning to the end. If it is a single-strand knot or if it a multi-strand knot such as a manrope knot or star knot, work each strand one at a time. It is better to tighten a complex knot two or three times, keeping the distortion to a minimum, rather than overtighten it and build in a distortion that you cannot get rid of. It is difficult to work slack back into part of a knot.

It can be difficult to guess how much rope is needed to make a knot, especially one of those knots that has many passes—such as the mats, the Turk's heads, and monkey's fist. It is a good idea to very roughly dummy the knot in your hand to get an idea of the sort of quantity needed. There can be no harm in measuring what you think you need, adding a little and making a note of the quantity you are going to use. After making the knot or mat, see what you have left and keep a record of the actual quantity and the size of rope used, together with the size of the finished knot or mat. Over time you will build up a better understanding of the amounts of rope needed.

Working with a long length of rope can be time consuming, and it can help if you pass the rope as a bight. Sometimes you may even make a bundle of the rope and pass that. This is particularly helpful when using fine line, especially with some of the plaits. Securing a bundle with a couple of half hitches or rubber bands will make things easier.

Where a knot or splice calls for the use of the actual strands of a three or four-strand rope, it will help if the ends of the strands are whipped or taped. It can also help if the ends are finished with different colours to help identify which is which. Take as much care as possible that the strand does not lose its lay and collapse when you are unlaying the rope. If the strand starts to break down, a gentle twist will help to put the lay back in the strand. You can use this same technique if the rope becomes unlaid by mistake. Twisting the strand will help put back that kink of rope that is needed for it to fit together with its fellow strand. This is very much the technique used in making the long splice and the grommet.

When you have made a splice as well as you can, with all the strands sitting well, the whole splice may be rolled underfoot to make it rounder still. When you cut the ends of a splice do not cut them too close as the first pull on the splice may cause the ends to pop out. It is far better to have the ends a little on the long side. Eventually they will wear away.

Left: A bundle held with half hitches (left) and one held by rubber bands.

Top Right: Cut ends.

Right: Laying a strand back.

Far Right: Rolling a splice underfoot.

The Knots

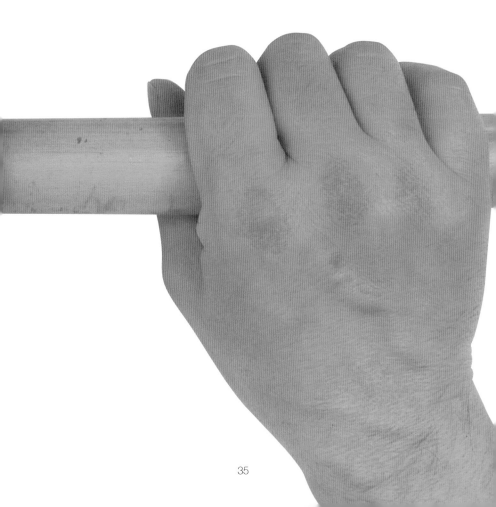

Stopper Knots

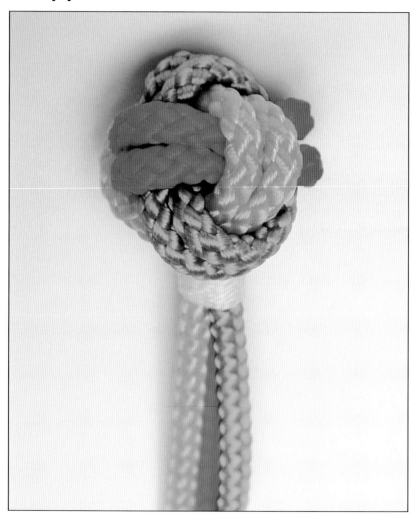

Stopper knots are tied at the end of a rope. They can be used to stop a rope pulling through a hole, or to stop the ends of a rope from fraying. They can provide a handhold, or give extra weight to the end of a rope to help when throwing it. They can be the simplest of knots or the most complex and decorative.

Index of Stopper Knots

Overhand Knot

This, the most basic of knots, is also known as the simple or thumb knot. As a stopper knot it is very compact, but after any strain is applied it is difficult to untie, especially in fine material. It sometimes has the habit of tying itself when not wanted. Look out for this, because an overhand knot in the middle of a length of rope will reduce the strength of the rope by about half. You should be aware of this if you choose to deliberately put a series of overhand knots in a length of rope to increase your grip. A series of double overhand knots tied on a fringe can give a beaded appearance.

The form of the overhand knot turns up inside many other more complicated knots, such as the water knot, fisherman's knot and true lover's knot.

It is worth pointing out that every knot has its mirror image. It is possible to reverse every move, so where there is an over an under is made instead, and visa versa; this gives an exact mirror image of the original knot. Sometimes the two knots will be referred to as the left and right-hand versions of the knot. This does not mean that they have been tied by a left or right-handed person.

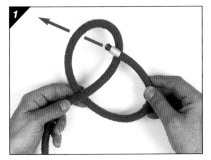

1   Make a crossing turn with the working end passing under the standing part of the rope.

2   Tuck the working end down through the middle of the loop formed by the crossing turn and out of the loop.

3   Pull both ends to tighten the knot. As it is being tightened the position of the knot can be moved nearer the end if so required.

4   This shows the two mirror versions of the overhand knot.

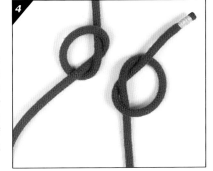

ARROWS

Throughout this book I have included arrows on the photographs where I felt it would be helpful to understand the next step to be taken in tying the knot. For example, the arrow in photo 1 above shows the action required for step 2. Photo 2 shows the completion of the action. I have kept these arrows to a minimum.

Slipped Overhand Knot

If the working end is not pulled right through when making the overhand knot, a bight or loop will be left giving a knot that can more easily be untied or "slipped," by pulling the short tail that has been left sticking out of the knot.

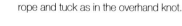

1 Form a bight in the working part of the rope and tuck as in the overhand knot.

2 The tightened knot.

Double Overhand Knot

Start as you would the overhand knot, but go on to make an extra tuck, and with a little manipulation as you pull the knot tight, you will have a larger stopper with a neat appearance.

By making even more tucks and careful manipulation, a slightly longer knot can be formed. The infamous cat-o'-nine tails whip is said to have three knots on every lash; as this knot is also known as a blood knot it is possible that double overhand knots were used.

1 Make a crossing turn with the working end passing under the standing part of the rope. Tuck the working end down through and out of the loop.
2 Tuck the working end a second time down and through the middle of the loop formed by the crossing turn and out of the loop.
3 As the knot is being tightened, work the turns of the knot into a smooth even knot with the fingers.

Capuchin Knot

French monks of the Capuchin order used this knot on the ends of their cord belts. This is a very long extended double overhand knot that is best tied in a different way to reduce the amount of manipulation needed to get it into a good shape. If a line is to be thrown, tying this knot at the end of the rope will make things a little easier, as it adds weight on the end of a heaving line.

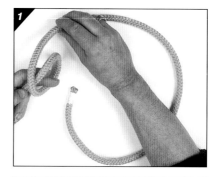

1 Holding the standing part of the rope in one hand, wrap the working part of the rope round the fingers.

2 Make four or five more turns, working round back down the fingers.

3 Take out your fingers leaving a sort of tunnel.

4 Tuck the working end through the tunnel formed by the fingers.

5 Pull tight ensuring that the turns of the knot sit neatly together, working out any slack in the knot.

Figure-of-Eight Knot

Very simple and quick to tie, this knot is far superior to the overhand knot, being both a little bulkier yet far easier to untie even after a strain has been put on the knot. It makes an ideal stopper and is used universally by yachtsmen to prevent their ropes pulling through blocks, eyebolts, and fairleads.

1 Make a crossing turn with the working end passing under the standing part of the rope and then bring the working end over the standing part.

2 Now tuck the working end up through the loop from behind, forming a figure of eight. Pull tight.

3 The finished knot.

Slipped Figure-of-Eight Knot

By leaving a bight rather than pulling the working end right through when making the figure-of-eight knot, a slightly bulkier knot is formed that can be easily untied or "slipped" by a tug on the short end.

1 Start as the figure-of-eight knot but tuck a bight formed in the working part of the rope.

Long Single Strand Plait

Looping the line to give three strands and then plaiting, pulling the free end through whenever possible, creates what is essentially a three-strand plait at the end of a piece of rope. There are two basic starts—one an overhand knot, the other a figure-of-eight. They will give knots of slightly different length. It is a fine decorative finish to the end of a piece of cordage. It is possible with care to tie these long single strand plaits in the middle of a rope or cord to make a decorative lanyard or curtain hold back.

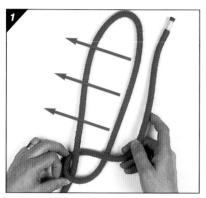

OVERHAND KNOT START

1　Make a loop and bring the working end over the standing end, then tuck up through the loop giving an overhand knot.
2　Twist the loop by bringing the right-hand side over the left-hand side of the loop.
3　Tuck the working end up through the loop.
4　Twist the loop again, this time bringing left over right, and then tuck up. Keep on repeating as many times as required.
5　The finished knot.

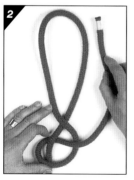

FIGURE-OF-EIGHT START

1 Make a loop with the working end, pass it under the standing part of the rope and then bring the working end over the standing part and up through the loop. Carry on as stages 2, 3, and 4 of the overhand version.

2 The finished knot.

Oysterman's Stopper Knot

Trailing from an oyster boat, Clifford Ashley, the author of *The Ashley Book of Knots*, saw what he thought was a new knot, and he set about copying it; this is the result. However, when he came to actually untie the knot he had seen, it turned out to just be a simple figure-of-eight knot tied in a very old and frayed piece of rope. This happy accident gives us another bulky stopper knot to use.

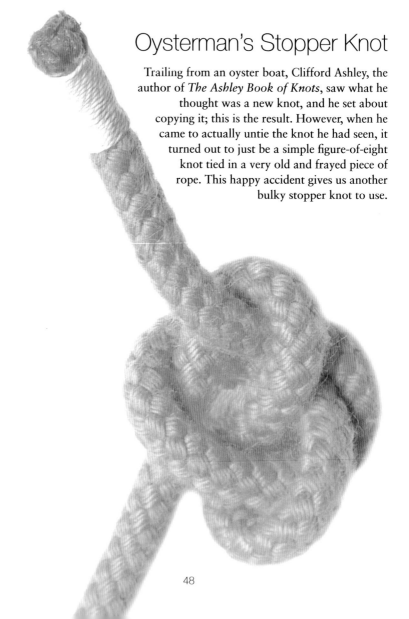

1. Make a crossing turn with the standing part on top.
2. Pull a bight of the standing part up through the loop.
3. Put short working end in the bight, and then pull tight.
4. The finished knot.

Sink Stopper Knot

This beauty of a stopper knot is just the job when a really large knot is wanted. It is a development of a slipped overhand knot but with the bight formed in the standing part. It does, however, need careful manipulation and tightening to ensure it keeps its shape and bulk.

1 Make a crossing turn with the working end passing under the standing part of the rope. Make a bight in the standing part.

2 Tuck the bight formed in the standing part up through the loop.

3 Tighten a little and take the working part in a counterclockwise direction round the standing part.

4 Tuck the working end through the bight, ensuring that the working part fits snugly into the crossing part of the original overhand knot. Work all slack out to form a neat tight knot.

5 The finished knot.

Monkey's Fist Knot

The monkey's fist has a special significance to sailors because it is often the first thing that connects them with the land at the end of a voyage.

To get heavy ropes from ship to shore or ship to ship, sailors first throw a light rope, a heaving line that is then used to pull the heavier rope across. To give weight to the heaving line, this beautiful big round knot is often used. When the knot has been made, but not tightened up, something has to be put inside the knot to give it shape and extra weight. Either the end of the rope is tied into a smaller stopper knot, such as the sink stopper, and tucked inside, or a heavy weight such as nut, ball bearing, or a stone is used. Care should be taken that the finished knot is not so heavy as to be dangerous to the people ashore. If it hits them, it might even get cut off !

This knot is a favorite knot to make a decorative key fob.

1   Wrap the rope round your hand three full clockwise turns. Prepare to make the next three turns at 90° to this first set of turns by turning the rope so it points away from you.

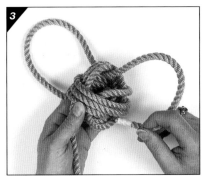

2 The rope now makes three full turns around the first set of turns. Note that as the turns are made, they come down the original set.

3 Tuck the end through the bottom space, round and through the top space, this will start the last set of turns which are at 90° to the set you have just made. Complete the turns to give three full turns.

4 You should now have three passes of rope on each face.

5 Open out a small hole where the working end came out and put in something spherical, to give the knot shape.

6 If you wish you can bury the working end in the center of the monkey's fist, before working the slack out of the knot, making the whole a tight sphere.

7 The finished knot.

Crown Knot

The crown knot is the simplest of the knots tied with the actual strands of three or four-strand rope. It gives a flat end to the rope and is the start of the back splice. It is also an important component in the making of many other more complex and decorative stopper knots, as well as a series of interesting plaits or sennits. The thing to remember when making the crown knot is that, when finished, each strand is doing the same as the others and that all strands point downward. Notice also that the strands should be pointing down in a counterclockwise direction if you are using the usual Z-laid rope, which certainly lays better and is essential if you wish to continue to go on and make a back splice.

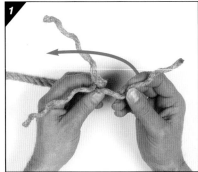

1 Unlay the rope a short way, and open out into a three-pointed pattern as the strands come out from the rope.
2 Take the right-hand strand and lay it across the top strand, making a small loop.
3 Bring the top strand over the first strand and down by the third strand.
4 The third strand comes over the second strand and tucks through the loop left in the first strand This forms an interlinked triangle, the crown knot.
5 The finished knot.

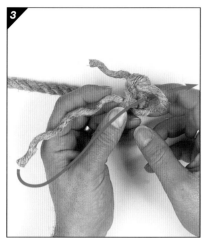

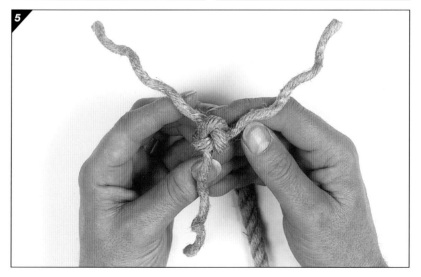

Double Crown Knot

By starting with a loosely tied crown knot and bringing each of the ends down the middle, a double crown knot is made. This gives a larger swelling to the end, increasing the amount of grip if you choose to use this as the start of a back splice.

Some people find it a great help to see where exactly each of the strands should go by making up a bundle of three different colored cords to simulate three-stranded rope.

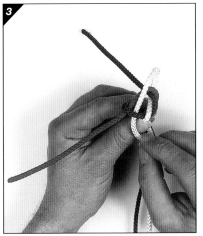

1 Make a crown knot (sees page 54–55).

2 Tuck one of the strands round and down through the middle of the crown and out past the side of the next strand round in a counterclockwise direction.

3 Repeat with the strand you have just tucked past. Take round and down through the middle and out past the side of the next strand in a counterclockwise direction.

4 Do the same with the remaining strand.

5 The double crown is now tied. Work tight and even; note that all the strands have followed similar paths.

Wall Knot

The wall knot is the opposite of the crown knot. While all strands are doing the same thing, this time they are pointing upward. In fact, if you turn the rope upside down, you could say that you have a crown, it all depends on how you make the tucks, and how you look at the finished knot. The wall knot is the basis of a number of other more complex stopper knots, sometimes being combined with the crown knot as well.

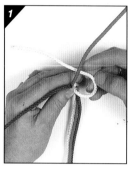

1. Unlay the rope a short way, and open out into a three-pointed pattern as the strands come out from the rope. Bring the lower strand round behind the top strand In a counterclockwise direction, leaving a small loop for later.
2. Bring the top strand down round behind the first strand and the third strand.
3. Bring the third strand down behind the second strand, round and up through the loop left in the first strand.
4. Work tight into a regular triangle. All of the working ends of the strands should point up.

Double Wall Knot

Starting with the wall knot, an extra pass is made by each of the strands. Take care that each strand follows a similar path to its neighbor. The double wall knot that results is a flat disc-like knot. We are lucky that an example from the very beginning of the nineteenth century has been preserved on the top bolt rope of the fore-top sail of HMS *Victory*. Knots, rope, and canvas are such ephemeral materials that any knot preserved from our past is of great significance, showing, as it does, exactly how our forefathers used to work with rope.

1   Make a wall knot. Take one of the strands.

2   Bring this strand round past the next or second strand in a counterclockwise direction. Bring it up through the hole that the second strand sticks up through.

Continued on page 60.

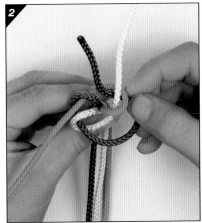

3 Bring the second strand past the third strand and up through the hole the third strand sticks up through.

4 Repeat the same action with the third or final strand, being careful to see that it passes up past where the first strand exited. Each strand will now have made the same passes and the knot should be symmetrical. Carefully work tight.

5 The finished knot.

Matthew Walker Knot

This is probably the earliest known knot named after a person. Exactly who Matthew Walker was is a mystery. When, in 1808, Darcy Lever published his *Young Sea Officer's Sheet Anchor*, he called this knot Matthew Walker's Knot, as though he was very well known at that time—so it is possible he was a rigger in one of the Royal Naval dockyards in the late 1700s. Clifford Ashley in *The Ashley Book of Knots* tells the story of a sailor called Matthew Walker condemned to death. The judge offered him a pardon if he could tie a knot that the judge could neither tie nor untie. Matthew Walker unlaid part of a long length of rope, tied the knot that now bears his name, and relaid the rope back to its original state. The judge, unaware as to how the knot was made, was beaten and gave Matthew Walker his reprieve. It's a nice story, but one yet to be substantiated.

1 Start with a wall knot.

Continued on page 62.

61

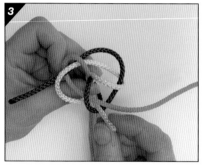

2   Tuck one strand through and up the next loop, in a counterclockwise direction, making sure it is positioned to the outer part of the loop.

3   Now take the strand that was already in that loop and tuck it in the same manner through the next loop round.

4   Repeat with the next strand round, it should pop up through the loop from the first strand. There should only be one strand sticking up and out of each of the loops.

5   Take any strand and tuck it up through the next loop in a counterclockwise direction. This will be the loop formed by itself, and will form an overhand knot.

6   Repeat this same movement with the other two strands.

7   Tighten the knot by carefully pulling on each of the strands a little at a time, working the knot into an even shape with the fingers of the left hand as you go. When tight you may wish to re lay up the rope.

8   The finished knot.

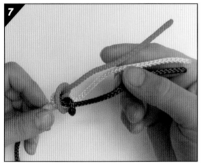

Single Matthew Walker Knot

1   Starting the same way as the full Matthew
    Walker, stop before the final round of
    tucks and you have what is known as a
    single Matthew Walker. It's slightly harder
    to work tight, but still a very fine stopper
    knot.

Manrope Knot

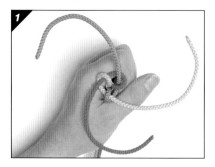

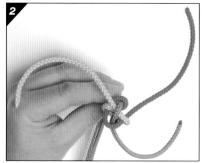

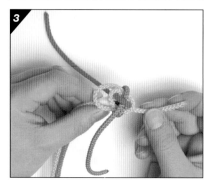

In the days of sail, the manrope was a rope that hung over the side of a vessel to help people climb aboard—and this knot was the favorite to be tied on its ends. Three or four-strand rope can be used. It starts with a wall knot, then a crown knot goes on top; the whole knot is then doubled to make a very handsome knot. For added effect the strands used to make this knot would be first covered with light canvas and then the knot would be painted in a selection of colors to show off the complexity of the design. Take care in working this knot tight, a bit at a time rather than all at once.

There is no better knot to be made at the end of a rope banister or barrier rope.

1 Start with a wall knot.
2 Make a crown knot on top.
3 Start to double the wall knot by following round the wall knot on the outside or lower part of the wall knot.
4 Repeat with each of the other strands.
5 Start to double the crown, by following round the crown on its lower edge.
6 Repeat with the other strands.
7 To finish tuck each strand down under the doubled wall.
8 Work tight and now the ends can be trimmed to finish off the knot.
9 The finished knot.

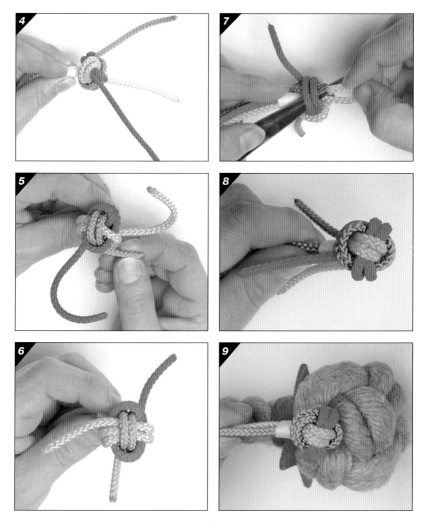

Diamond and Doubled Diamond Knot

First tie a crown knot, but do not work it tight; then tie a wall knot beneath; then tuck each strand up through the middle. Special care must be taken that these last tucks all follow a similar path. Treat all strands equally! The knot can now be worked tight, a bit at a time, making sure that the finished knot is good and symmetrical. The rope strands can be relaid up, or teased out to make a tassel. To make a bigger, more handsome knot, before the final series of tuck ups, follow the crown round so as to double it, then follow the wall round before the final tuck up through the middle.

This knot is splendid to decorate a knife or whistle lanyard, or to give a grip at the end of a rope used to pull a bucket on board ship.

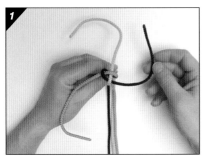

1 Start with a crown knot.
2 Tie a wall knot below the crown knot.
3 Tuck one end up through the middle of the crown. Make the tuck so the strand has passed round itself.
4 Repeat with the other two strands. They should all form a similar symmetric pattern. Pull tight to achieve a finished knot.

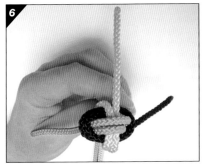

5 To double the diamond knot, rather than tucking up through the middle of the crown, double the crown, with each strand, by following by the side of the crown.

6 Repeat with the other two strands.

7 Now double the wall bringing the end of each strand up through the middle of the knot. Work the knot tight to finish.

8 The finished knot.

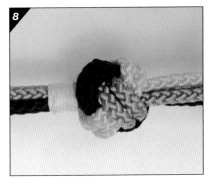

Star Knot

One of the pinnacles of the knot tyer's art, this knot is a challenge to all. It is tied in a minimum of four (to a maximum of eight) strands of rope or cord. The number of strands gives the number of points to the star. Some say that a five-pointed star should be made, one point for every ocean; others speak of seven points for the seven seas. I find that six works well as there are many

different six-strand sennits to choose from to make a start. Do not be daunted by its complexity, but look on it as a series of simple moves in a symmetrical pattern. Each layer of the knot needs to be worked into a fair shape as you go. Do not work it fully tight until the whole knot is finished. It is a great help to start with each strand being a differing color. Have courage, take it slowly, it is possible! When the knot is complete, the ends can be unlayed to make a tassel, or you could carry on with more sennit.

Alternatively, you can finish the star by tucking the ends back on themselves, either into the knot or by making a double crown.

1 Start with six strands either bound together or in a six-strand sennit (in this case a three + three-strand crown sennit).

2 Make a series of interlinked loops. These will form the points of the star.

3 Crown the strands in a clockwise direction, keep everything fairly tight and neat.

Continued on page 70.

4 Tuck each strand back on itself, repeating the underlaying pattern of the point of the star.

5 Lay out the strands so they follow the line of the crown made in step 3.

6 Now, in turn, tuck each strand down the small hole in the point of the star, tucking through both layers of the knot.

7 Turn the knot over so you can see the bottom of the knot and, in turn, lay the strand back on itself and tuck up to the middle of the knot. When all strands have been tucked, the star knot just requires systematically working tight. Do a little at a time.

8 Finished star looking from the side. Either carry on with your sennit, make a tassle, or finish with a double crown knot.

9 To finish with a double crown knot first make a crown knot, each strand inter-linking with the next. In turn, tuck each strand down through the middle of the star knot bringing each end out at a separate point around the lower part of the star. When all strands have been so tucked and pulled tight, they can be trimmed at the lower exit points.

10, 11 The finished knot. Well Done!!!

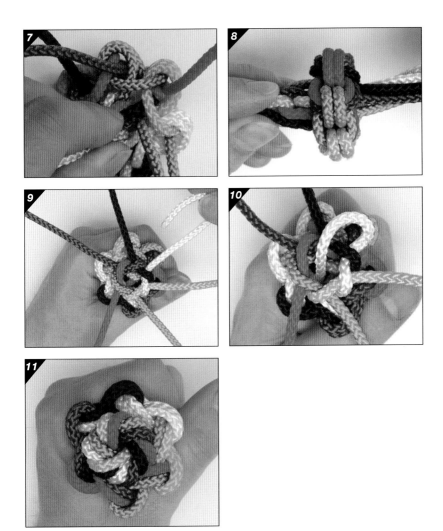

Whipping & Some Variations

A whipping is a binding of fine twine made at the end of the rope to prevent the rope from coming undone. From the simple whipping can be developed many variations that are either more secure or decorative.

Index of Whipping Knots

Simple Whipping

Sometimes called a common whipping, this is the easiest way to stop the end of any type of rope from fraying. It can also be used to mark the rope along its length. As with all whippings, make the turns as tight as possible. Take care when you come to bury the end as pulling fine whipping twine can easily cut the finger; it will help to wrap the twine round a spike rather than your finger, better still use a marlinespike hitch (see page 128). This same simple whipping can also be used to fix the rings to a fishing rod, or stop the end of a tool handle splitting.

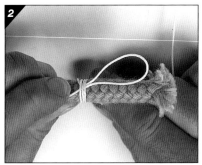

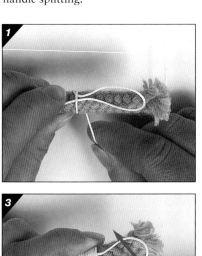

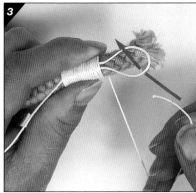

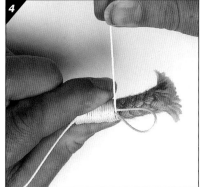

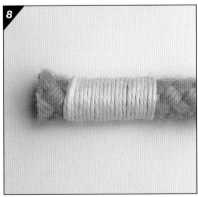

1 Make a bight in the whipping twine and wrap round the base of the bight. There should be a short tail coming out from under the binding.

2 Continue to make tight turns round the rope, working up toward the end of both the bight and the rope.

3 When the wrapped turns of the whipping twine form a long enough whipping, pull extra tight. There should still be a bight sticking out of the whipping.

4 Tuck the working end of the whipping twine through the bight.

5 Keeping tension on the working end of the whipping twine, pull the short tail so as to trap the working part.

6 By pulling very hard on the tail the trapped working part will be pulled into the middle of the whipping.

7 Trim the ends of the whipping and the rope.

8 The finished whipping.

West Country Whipping

First described by George Biddlecombe in *The Art of Rigging* in 1848, the best use for this whipping is to hold together the ends of a large rope or cable. The very first knot stops any movement of the rope ends. The series of overhand knots tied round the rope, working back from the end and finished off with a reef knot, ensures that, should the whipping start to come undone, it will take a good while before failing completely—and the loose ends of the whipping will draw attention to the problem so it can be repaired before any harm can occur.

1 In the middle of the whipping twine, tie
   the first part of an overhand knot round
   the end of the rope.
2 Bring the ends of the whipping twine
   behind the rope and tie another overhand
   knot.
3 Repeat again at the front of the rope.
4 Continue to make this series of overhand
   knots front and back until the full length of
   the whipping has been made.
5 Finish with a reef knot.

French Whipping

This series of half hitches works in much the same way as the West Country whipping but looks a lot neater. Again it is recommended that the hitches are worked back from the end of the rope.

A long length of French whipping, made round a tool handle or ship's wheel, will give a decorative finish with a good grip. Take care if you are making a long length, as you are sure to get sore fingers!

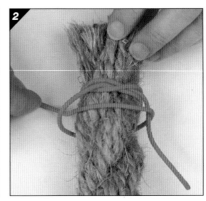

1 Start with a clove hitch or constrictor knot round the end of the rope. One end of the whipping twine should be short, the other long.

2 With the long end make a half hitch round the rope trapping the short end.

3 Continue to make a series of half hitches round the rope. Work away from the end of the rope until the whipping is long enough, pulling each half hitch as tight as possible.

4 Tie an overhand knot in the end of the whipping twine and work it as close to the last half hitch as possible. This should stop the hitches working loose.

Palm and Needle Whipping on Braided Rope

Braided rope, especially that with some kind of core, needs a whipping that will both stop the end fraying and also stop the cover moving in relation to the core itself. On a yacht the ends of braided rope take a great deal of punishment, so a very secure whipping is called for. Although a palm and needle whipping may take a little trouble to make and needs both a sailmaker's palm and a needle, the finished whipping is very secure, looks good, and is highly recommended.

If you have the time there is no harm in making a second whipping a few inches back from the first whipping.

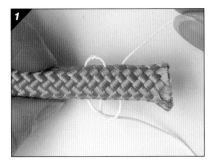

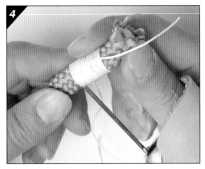

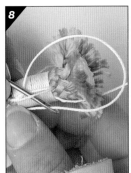

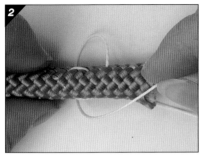

1 Stitch through the rope a couple of times working towards the end of the rope and catching the loose end of the twine so it will not pull out.

2 Now start to wrap the twine tightly round the rope.

3 Work the wrapping back from the end until the whipping is long enough.

4 Push the needle in to the rope at the base of the whipping and out directly opposite.

5 Bring the twine straight up to the top of the whipping and push straight through the rope down the other side of the whipping and trough the rope again, coming out at the first entry point.

6 Repeat this so there are two strands of twine on both sides of the whipping.

7, 8 Finish the whipping as a seizing (see page 86) then trim end of rope.

9 Finished palm and needle whipping on braided rope.

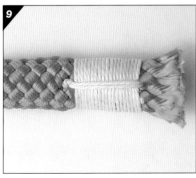

Palm and Needle Whipping on Three-Strand Rope

Made in much the same way as the palm and needle whipping for braided rope, this creates a beautiful looking and very secure whipping. Again, this whipping can also be made a few inches back from the first or end whipping.

1. Stitch through the rope a couple of times working toward the end of the rope and catching the loose end of the twine so it will not pull out.
2. Now start to wrap the twine tightly round the rope.
3. Work the wrapping back from the end until the whipping is long enough.
4. Push the needle into the rope at one of the grooves of the rope and out at another.

5. Now follow the groove of the rope to the end and push the needle in and out at the start of the next groove.
6. Repeat this until all the grooves have a piece of line in them, and then carry on until they each have two pieces of line laying in them.
7. Finish the whipping as a seizing (see page 86) then trim end of rope.
8. Finished palm and needle whipping on three-strand rope.

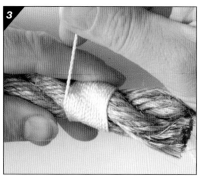

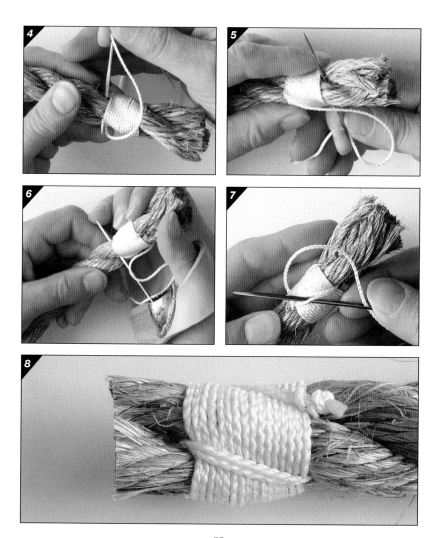

Sailmaker's Whipping

The sailmaker's whipping has all the appearance of the palm and needle whipping but is made without the use of either palm or needle. It is very secure, but can only be made at the end of three-strand rope. When you start this whipping, take care not to lose the lay of the rope as you put the first loop between the strands. Always finish with a reef knot pulled tight.

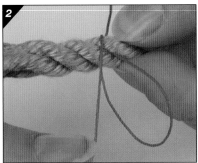

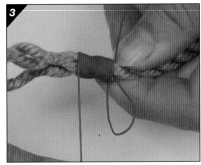

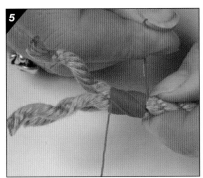

1. Open out the strands at the end of the rope, keeping as much lay in the strands as possible. Put a loop of whipping twine round one of the strands and the working and standing ends of the whipping twine out of the space between the other two strands.

2. Lay the strands of the rope back again, and make a turn round the rope with the working end of the whipping twine. Leave the short standing end and the loop of twine to stand free.

3. Keep on wrapping the whipping twine tightly round the rope, working toward the rope's end.

4. Bring the loop of twine up over the end of the strand that it was round. The whipping line should follow the path of the groove in the rope.

5. Pull the short standing end to tighten the loop round its strand.

6. Take the short standing end that you have just pulled on up to the top following the groove in the rope.

7. Tie the standing and working ends together with a reef knot in the center of the rope.

8. Trim the ends to finish the whipping.

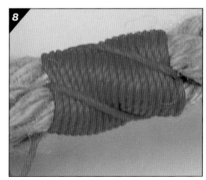

Seizing

A seizing is a kind of long whipping made round two pieces of rope. It is often used to form an eye in a piece of rope. A great deal of friction is generated by the tightness of the seizing, and a series of well-made seizings are capable of taking immense strain. For hundreds of years the shrouds, those heavy ropes used to support the masts of sailing ships, were finished off with a series of seizings. For very large shrouds made of steel rope the seizing would be made with wire but made in the same manner.

It is important that each turn of the seizing is pulled as tight as possible and lies close to the previous turn.

1   Make a constrictor knot round both pieces of rope.
2   Wrap tightly round away from the end and over the short tail left from the constrictor knot.
3   When enough wrapping is done pull extra tight.
4   Put the working end between the "legs" of the two pieces of rope, and then down the other end of the seizing. These are frapping turns.

5   Make two complete sets of frapping
    turns.

6   Tuck the working end under the first of
    the frapping turns, tucking the end out
    from between the two frapping turns.

7   Bring the line round in a loop and tuck
    under the second frapping turn, tucking
    from the outside into the middle. This
    hitch will lock off the seizing.

8   Pull the locking hitch tight and finish the
    twine with an overhand knot to stop any
    chance of the end working out.

9   The finished seizing.

Stitch and Seize

It can be very difficult to make a permanent loop at the end of a piece of braided rope. By first stitching the rope together, then putting a tight seizing over the stitching, a strong eye can be made. You will need to use a sailmaker's palm and needle to make the stitches. It is a very good idea to make an extra locking stitch halfway along the binding turns as additional security. Should one part break, the other half of the seizing should hold long enough to allow a repair to be made. As always, make all the binding turns as tight as possible.

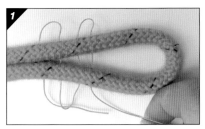

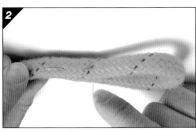

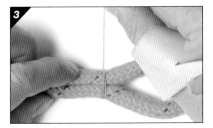

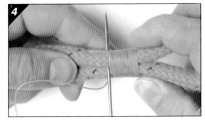

1 Fold the rope back and stitch through the two pieces of the rope, catching the tail of the twine so it will not pull out.
2 Pull tight.
3 Start to wrap tightly round the ropes working back over the stitching.
4 When half the wrapping has been made, make a stitch through the rope.
5 Bring the twine round the rope and stitch down through the other piece of rope before carrying on with the wrapping turns.
6 Bring the twine round and up between the two pieces of rope and then go on to make two frapping turns.
7 Finish as a seizing (see page 86).
8 The finished seizing.

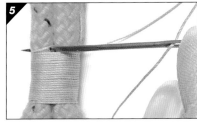

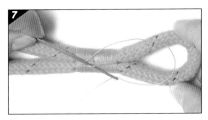

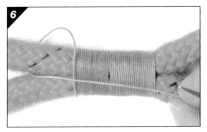

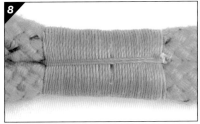

Moku Hitching

Moku hitching gives a very decorative grip to a handle or ship's wheel. It could be thought of as two lots of French whipping (see page 78) each going in opposite directions. Start with a constrictor knot (see page 107) in the middle of the line and work the hitches in alternate directions. It is not possible to add extra line neatly as you go along, so it is worth taking the trouble to dummy up a short length, and work out how much will be needed to cover the total length.

Then, to be on the safe side, add a little extra, as the actual job may make up a little tighter and closer than your dummy run.

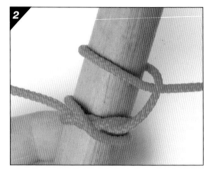

1 Start with a constrictor knot in the middle of the line.
2 With the line that points out to the right of the constrictor knot make a half hitch to the right by bringing the line round the pole and under itself.
3 With the other line, exiting to the left, make a half hitch to the left.
4 Continue hitching to right then left.
5 The hitches will eventually meet at the back of the pole.
6 At the meeting point, carry on hitching whichever strand is next over the other strand.
7 Carry on until the full amount of Moku hitching is finished.

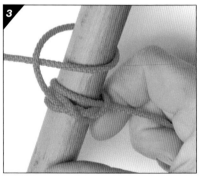

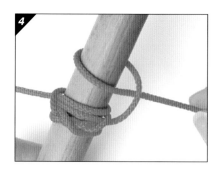

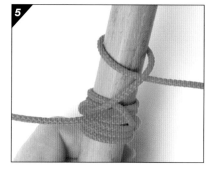

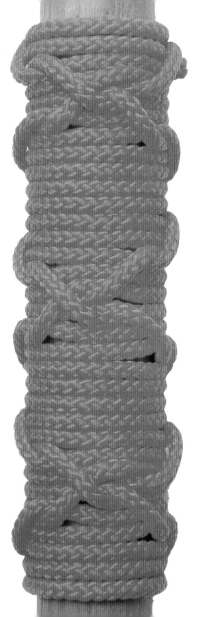

Ringbolt Hitching

1 Tie three strands of line to the pole using a constrictor knot (see page 107).
2 Hitch the middle strand to the right.
3 Hitch the right-hand strand to the left, then the left-hand strand to the right.
4 Hitch what was the first strand and is now furthest away from the end. As this strand stuck out to the right, hitch to left
5 Hitch the furthest back strand in the opposite direction to which it stuck out.
6 Continue until the required amount of ring bolt hitching is completed.

In the days before chain mooring cables—the heavy hemp anchor cables—were made fast with a series of ropes to ringbolts set in the deck of the ship. To prevent wear and chafe, these rings were wrapped with cordage. The outer circumference being greater than the inner part of the ring, simply wrapping the line would leave gaps and have a tendency to work loose. By using three strands and hitching them in alternate directions, this will be overcome. Carefully done, this gives an outer rim that has detailing looking like a three-strand sennit ridge. Sometimes this ringbolt hitching is called "cockscombing" because of this detail. Whatever name is used, this is a fine way to cover any item that is round and curved at the same time, be it

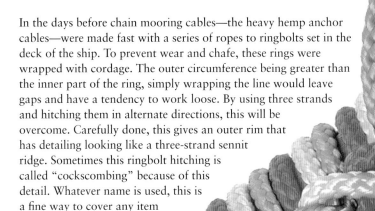

ringbolt, eyebolt, or the handle on a kettle. For the very best effect ensure that the ridge is straight and does not roll to one side or the other.

St. Mary's Hitching

This variation on the French hitching theme was found by Brion Toss. He named it after a fine little church in Anacortes, Washington. The hitches in the three strands are always made in the same direction. Care should be taken to ensure that they lay neatly in place to give the spiraling rope effect.

Do a dummy run before the main job so you can be certain you have enough line to finish the job.

1. Tie three strands of line to the pole with a constrictor knot (see page 107).
2. With the left-hand strand make a half hitch to the right.
3. Take the next strand and hitch to the right.
4. Take the last strand and hitch to the right.
5. The first strand is again hitched to the right and the cycle continues.
6. The finished length of St. Mary's hitching.

Binding Knots

Usually tied round an object or bundle, the binding knot can be tightened to hold itself in place. It is not for joining two separate ropes together, as it can easily come undone when there is no tension on the knot.

Index of Binding Knots

Reef or Square Knot

This is not a knot for joining ropes together but for tying the two ends of a binding around an object. For the sailor that object would be the bundle of sail that is formed when a reef is put in. A tug on one of the working ends and the knot will collapse and be able to be slid apart. The ancient Greeks and Romans believed that this knot was invented by the god Hercules; they thought that it had many magic powers, including the ability to heal wounds quickly. It is still the best knot to tie together the end of a bandage or sling because it lies square or flat—the second half of the knot is always made in the opposite direction to the first part, to ensure that it lies like this.

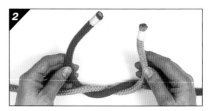

1. Put the left-hand working end on top of the right-hand working end.
2. Bring the left-hand working end under the right-hand working end.
3. Put the working end that is now on the right on top of the working end that is now on the left.
4. Bring the working end that is on top over and then under the other working end so that the working end you are moving comes out of the same space that it entered the knot. Pull tight.
5. The finished knot.

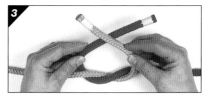

Slipped Reef or Bow Knot

In the same way that the overhand knot can be turned into a slipped overhand by using a bight or loop instead of the working end, so the reef can be turned into a quick release knot. Using bights instead of the plain working ends in the second half of the reef knot, a slipped version, sometimes called a "bow," is made. This knot can be easily untied or "slipped," by pulling the short tails that have been left sticking out of the knot.

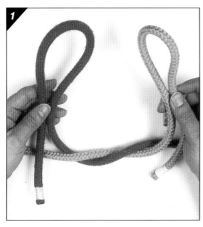

1 Start as a reef knot but then form loops or bights in each end.
2 Tuck the right bight over the left bight and under making the slipped reef.
3 The finished knot.

Granny Knot

When trying to make a reef knot and failing to make the second part correctly, i.e. not making it square to the first part, the result is a granny knot, hard to undo when wanted, yet not secure. See how the working ends poke out at right angles to the knot. It is said that this is how gorillas tie the creepers that make up their nests, so perhaps this should be called a gorilla rather than a granny!

1 The same start as a reef knot, left over right and under.
2 The left-hand working end comes over the right-hand working end and under.
3 The finished knot.

Thief Knot

The thief knot is similar in shape and form to the reef knot, but with the working ends coming out on opposite sides of the knot. This difference is not so obvious unless you are looking for it. When pilfering of stores was suspected, the thief knot would be tied round a sack or bag. Having untied the thief knot, the unsuspecting rogue would tie the bag up with a reef knot making his illicit activity obvious. The tying of this knot should help you understand the making of knots, their shape, and form. Apart from that and the chance to tell a knotty story, the thief knot is of little use to anyone.

1 Make a loop in the left-hand rope with the short end on top, and hold. Put the right-hand working end through the loop.
2 Bring what was the right-hand working end round the short end and down behind the loop.
3 Bring the working end through the loop formed in the left-hand rope, giving a similar pattern and form to a reef knot but with the short ends on opposite sides of the knot.

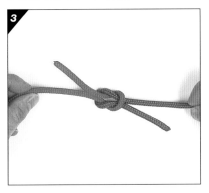

Surgeon's Knot

The surgeon's knot is based on the reef knot but with extra turns. When tying off sutures inside the body, surgeons use forceps to make this knot, but for everyday use, in everyday materials, hands and fingers do the perfect job. Start as the reef knot but make an extra tuck which holds the knot in place in readiness for the second or top part of the finished knot. There may be either one finishing tuck on top like the reef or two like the lower part of the knot. The surgeon's knot is a useful knot to have to tie up those hard to control bundles like a rolled up tent, foam mattress or a really squashy parcel.

1 Start as a reef knot but then tuck the left-hand working end a second time.
2 Tuck what is now the right-hand working end over and under the left-hand working end.
3 Make a second tuck with the left-hand working end.
4 Pull tight. Note that the surgeon's knot is flat like a reef knot.
5 The finished knot.

Turquoise Turtle

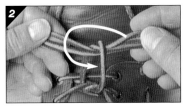

Named by Brion Toss, after he saw it being used to tie up parcels in a boutique called "The Turquoise Turtle," this knot is probably the most perfect for tying up shoelaces. In fact, to some people this is known as the "Shoemaker's Knot." This knot can either start as a reef knot or as a surgeon's knot depending on the gap at the top of your shoe. The second half of the knot is a surgeon's knot tied with the loops as you would tie a reef bow. A little push with the thumb will make the middle part of the knot sit neat and tidy, holding your shoe tied tight all day. If you have made your Turquoise Turtle properly a tug on the short ends of the laces will cause the knot to come undone.

1. Start as if you are going to make a reef knot (see page 98) and form your laces into loops as if to make a slipped reef bow.

2. Tuck the right bight over the left bight and under, making the slipped reef. Keep a gap in the middle of the knot.

3. Take the right-hand bundle, consisting of loop and one end of the lace, and bring the entire bundle over and down through the gap you left in the middle of the bow.

4. Pull tight and as you are doing this work the right-hand crossing strand to the centre of the bow.

5. Complete by pulling tight.

Clove Hitch

Quick and easy to tie, the clove hitch consists of two half hitches or crossing turns, each made in the same direction. It is used to finish off knots like the round turn and two half hitches and the various types of lashing, as well as being a useful knot on its own. It makes an ideal crossing knot when staking and roping out an arena. Boaters often use the clove hitch to quickly moor a small boat to a bollard or post. This is not such a good idea, except perhaps as a very temporary measure, as it can easily work loose. An extra half hitch round the standing part helps to stop this, but there are better knots to use, such as the round turn and two half hitches or the bowline, depending on the circumstances.

Method # 1 (Left)

This is the way to make the clove hitch in the middle of a piece of rope, but it must be slipped over the top of the post, pole, or bollard.

1   In the middle of the rope make a crossing turn or half hitch, with the rope that comes from the left being on top.
2   To the right of the first crossing turn make a half hitch, with exactly the same configuration.
3   Put the right-hand half hitch on top of the left-hand half hitch.
4   The pair of hitches are now slipped over the top of the post.

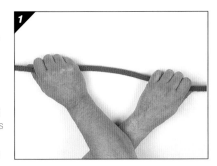

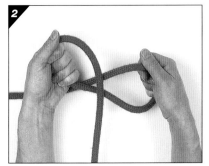

Method # 2 (Right)

One to impress your friends: a super quick version of method # 1, without letting go of the rope.

1   Cross your hands right over left and hold the rope.
2   Without letting go of the rope, uncross your hands.
3   Put the turn in your right hand on top of the turn in your left hand—you now have a clove hitch to place over whatever you like.

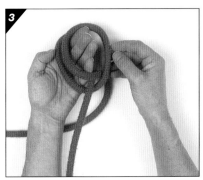

Method # 3

If you wish to learn only one method, then this is the one, as it can be used in all circumstances. It is the only way if there is no access to the end of the pole, post or rail. Make sure that the hitches go in the same direction and do not make a cow hitch, which is even less secure.

1 Make a turn round the post bringing the working end of the rope over and trapping the standing part of the rope—this makes the first half hitch.
2 Bring the working end round behind the post, above the first half hitch.
3 Put the working end under the turn just made. This gives the second half hitch forming the clove hitch.
4 The finished knot.

Constrictor Knot

This is a very useful development from the clove hitch. With just one extra tuck you have a knot that can be tightened round any object. Made in fine twine it makes an ideal quick provisional whipping on the end of a cut length of rope. It will do the job of a temporary hoseclip, or a round clamp when gluing up a split in a round piece of wood. A really tight knot can be made if the ends of the line are pulled with the line held round a spike or screwdriver, preferably with a marlinespike hitch. But be warned! It grabs so tightly that it is very hard to undo; you may have to resort to a spike or even a knife.

1 Start with a clove hitch.
2 Bring the working end tuck over and under the standing part, making the first half of a reef knot.
3 Pull tight so that the half knot is trapped under the crossing of the clove hitch to finish the knot.

Packer's Knot

Used by people packing all kinds of boxes, bundles, parcels, and packages, the very best version of this knot is based on the figure-of-eight knot, but an overhand knot works nearly as well. The knot with the end tucked through forms a running loop or noose and as it is tightened round a bundle, the friction starts to grip until the knot is as tight as it will go. As long as the string is not very slippery, it will hold tight. To be on the safe side, it is best to put a locking half hitch round the end after tightening. If the package needs it, a number of these bands can be made individually or the string can be taken round the package at right angles, coming back to the packers knot, where it can be tied off with a couple of half hitches.

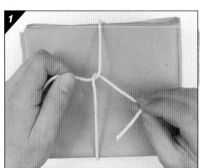

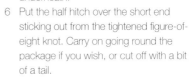

1   Pass your packing twine round the package, and bring the working end round and under the standing part.

2   Bring the working end over and then under the working part, as if making a figure-of-eight knot.

3   Finish off the figure-of-eight knot.

4   Pull on the standing part and the figure-of-eight knot will tighten round the twine and cause the figure-of-eight knot to grip.

5   To lock the packer's knot make a half hitch with the standing part leaving from underneath.

6   Put the half hitch over the short end sticking out from the tightened figure-of-eight knot. Carry on going round the package if you wish, or cut off with a bit of a tail.

Bends

A bend is used to join together two pieces of rope temporarily. Although most bends are only suitable for joining together ropes of the same size, there is at least one suitable for ropes of differing sizes (see page 113). Bends made in very fine line may prove difficult to untie.

Index of Bending Knots

Sheet Bend

The sheet bend is one of the simplest and best ways of joining two pieces of rope together. It is quick and easy to tie. It works well if the ropes are the same or almost the same size. If there is any substantial difference of rope size, then use the double sheet bend. The sheet bend has been known to mankind for many thousands of years. The oldest knot found was a sheet bend, in a fragment of fishing net, which has been dated to be 9,000 years old.

1 Fold the end of a piece of rope back on itself to form a bight. If the ropes to be joined are of varying sizes then this should be the larger of the two. Bring the working end of the second piece of rope up through the bight.

2 Take the working end of the rope round the shorter end of the first rope and on round behind the standing part.

3 The working end of the second piece of rope is tucked under itself. Then pull tight.

4 The finished knot.

Double sheet bend

If there is any substantial variation of rope size then use the double sheet bend. Made with the thinner of the two pieces of rope, the extra turn in the double sheet bend makes a lot of difference. The extra turn stops any slipping, or the knot collapsing.

1   Make a sheet bend, then carry on and make a second pass right round the bight with the working end of the second piece of rope.
2   The finished knot.

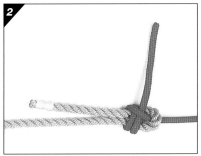

Slipped sheet bend

By tucking a bight of rope rather than an end, a quick release version of the sheet bend is made. As with any slipped version of a knot, care should be taken to ensure that the knot is properly formed with the slip loop jammed in place.

Carrick Bend

The design and form of the carrick bend is known all over the world. As well as being used to join ropes together, it is the basis of many other decorative knots. The carrick bend is perhaps the most perfect, beautiful and symmetrical of bends. When making this bend be sure that the working ends are opposite one another and are not too short, as the bend will collapse when put under strain. It is also easily untied. In the past this bend was used to join very large cables, then it was kept flat with the ends seized to the standing part, so allowing the cable to go round a capstan or windlass.

6

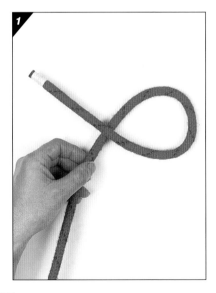

1

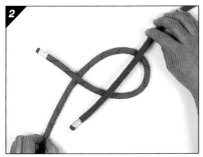

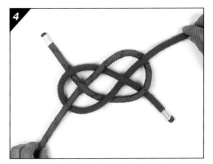

1. In the first rope make a loop with a crossing turn, the short end to be on top.
2. Put the second rope on top of the loop, the standing end to be opposite to the standing end of the first rope.
3. Take the working end of the second rope round behind the standing part of the first rope and then over the short end.
4. The working end of the second rope goes under the first rope, over itself, and under the first rope again. This gives the full over and under pattern of the carrick bend.
5. The finished knot collapsed.
6. At far left can be seen the finished knot with seized ends.

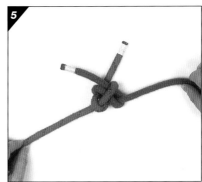

Fisherman's Knot

Consisting of sliding overhand knots tied round the standing part of the line, this is an ideal way of joining together two thin pieces of rope or line, although in finer line it can be difficult to untie. It is much used by anglers and climbers. Make certain that the ends of the overhand knots are long enough to allow for any slipping, that they lie neatly parallel to the standing part and do not stick out at right angles. If they do, retie so that they lie flat. When used for climbing, it is good practice to tape the ends down to the main body of the rope with adhesive tape, to avoid them slipping or being snagged. For slippery line use the double fisherman's knot.

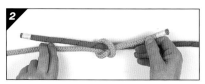

1 Lay the ropes alongside each other end to end. Take one of the ropes and bring it over the other and under itself.
2 Complete the overhand knot round the second rope.
3 Make an overhand knot round the standing part of the first rope.
4 Slide together to complete the knot.
5 The finished knot.
6 The fisherman's knot with taped ends.

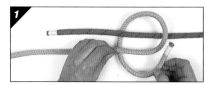

Double fisherman's knot

Ideal for slippery line, this version of the fisherman's knot is sometimes called the grapevine knot or the barrel knot. The overhand knots of the fisherman's knot are replaced with double overhand knots. This makes a very neat, almost beautiful knot.

1 With the first rope make a double overhand knot round the body of the second rope.
2 Make a double overhand knot round the body of the first rope; pull tight and slide together.
3 The finished knot.

Half-slipped fisherman's knot

By replacing one of the overhand knots with a slipped overhand knot it will be much easier to untie, but as with all slip knots you should be certain that the knot has been set properly and that there is no likelihood of the slipped end being pulled by accident.

4 Make one of the overhand knots a slipped overhand knot, the second overhand knot plain.

Water Knot

Once the favorite with anglers, this knot was mentioned in *Treatyse of Fyshing wyth an Angle* by Dame Juiana Berners, Prioress of Sopwell, printed in 1496. The water knot is another good knot for joining fine lines together. It, too, has an overhand at its heart. In the water knot, one overhand knot is followed round by the other overhand knot. Make sure that the lines lie neat and evenly. Today this knot is the correct knot for tying together the ends of the strong woven tape used by climbers, who often call this knot the tape knot.

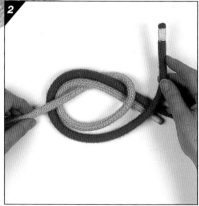

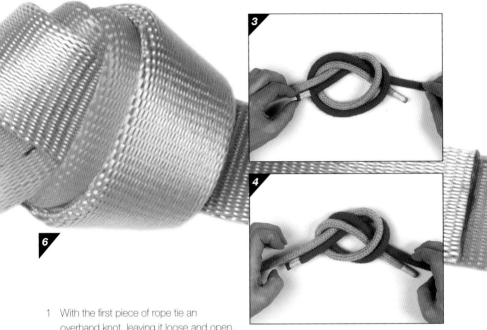

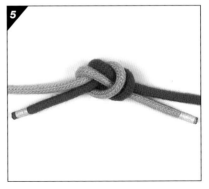

1 With the first piece of rope tie an overhand knot, leaving it loose and open.
2 Starting at the very end of the first piece of rope, follow round the overhand knot with the second piece of rope.
3 Complete the doubling of the overhand knot.
4 Holding both ends and starting parts of the rope, pull tight. Make sure as you do so that the doubled overhand knot is smooth and neat.
5 The finished knot.
6 Water knot tied in tape.

119

Blood Knot

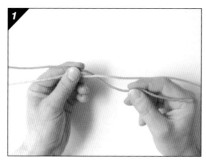

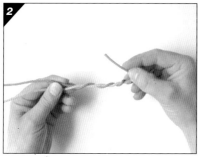

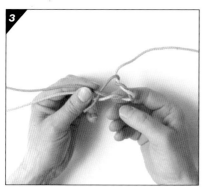

One of many knots with the name of blood knot, this one is sometimes called the barrel knot. It is used by anglers to join together their fine nylon lines. Before struggling to tie this knot in fine fishing line, try it in a thin cord. When made in fishing line, it is made with plenty of turns and it helps if the line is wetted in the mouth to lubricate the turns so they can work tight. Once tied and pulled tight it is almost impossible to undo; if you want to, you will have to resort to the knife.

1 Overlap the two pieces of line keeping them slightly apart in the left hand.
2 Wrap the working end of the left-hand line round the right-hand line giving an S-twist to the lines.
3 Tuck the working end of the line you have just wrapped up through the small gap kept open in you left hand.
4 Now twist the other working end round the standing part: this should continue to form an S-twist.
5 When you have as many twists as the first side, tuck back through the same place as the first end. The two ends should point out in opposite directions.

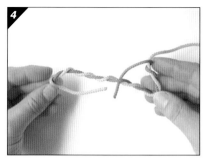

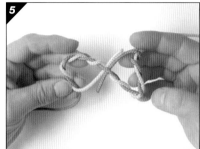

6 Pull tight, working the twists up close together. Make sure the ends do not pop out; they will work together easier in fishing line if the knot is wetted in the mouth.

7 The finished knot in fine cord shows well the two halves of the knot.

Hunter's Bend

This bend became world famous in 1978 when it appeared on the front page of *The Times* newspaper of London. It was discovered by Dr. Edward Hunter and was thought to be an entirely new knot, but as the news passed around the world it turned out that Phil Smith of California had described it in his book *Knots for Mountaineering* published in 1953. He called it the rigger's bend. All the correspondence generated by the publicity led to the foundation of the International Guild of Knot Tyers, now with well over 1,000 members worldwide. So it could be said that this is a bend for joining people together.

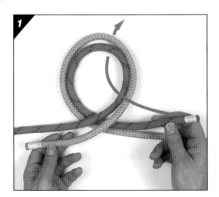

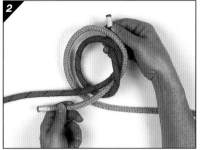

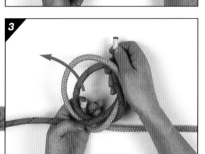

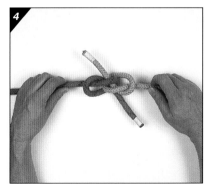

1. Lay the two ends of the rope together and then make a crossing turn keeping all neat and flat.
2. Tuck the right-hand end, which should be under the crossing of the turn, down through the loop already formed.
3. Bring the left-hand end, which was on top, round and up through the loop. Make sure that the right-hand end does not slip out of the loop.
4. Pull tight, ensuring that the short ends do not pop out.
5. The finished knot.

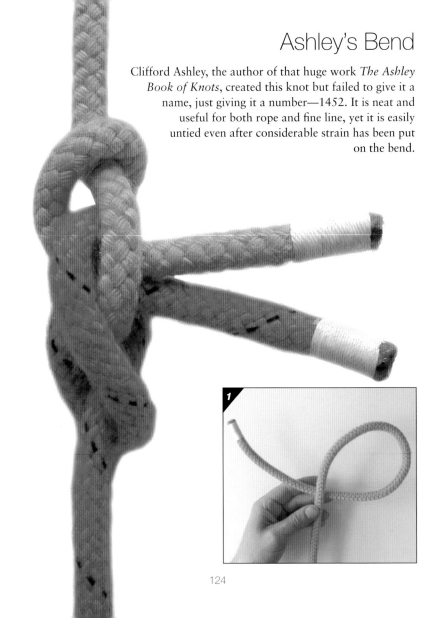

Ashley's Bend

Clifford Ashley, the author of that huge work *The Ashley Book of Knots*, created this knot but failed to give it a name, just giving it a number—1452. It is neat and useful for both rope and fine line, yet it is easily untied even after considerable strain has been put on the bend.

1

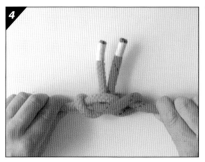

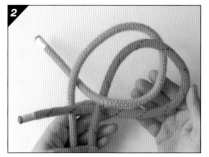

1 Make a crossing turn loop with the standing part on top.
2 Bring the working end of the second rope up through the center of the loop, round under itself and over the standing part of the first rope, making a similar loop to the first piece of rope.
3 Take the two working ends that are sticking out to the left and put them both through the center of the pair of loops.
4 Pull tight.
5 The finished knot.

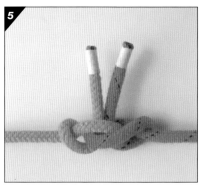

Hitches

Pocket Guide to Knots & Splices

Hitches are tied round or to something, they are generally quick to tie, and easy to untie. However care must be taken that the strain is put on the correct rope end and in the right direction.

Index of Hitch Knots

Marlinespike Hitch

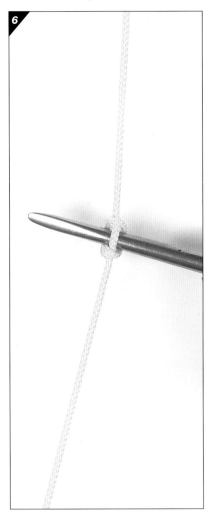

Almost magic, this hitch is named after the steel spike used to splice wire and rope, but it works perfectly well with any piece of round metal or wood—a screwdriver or broom handle, for example.

The marlinespike hitch enables you to pull a thin piece of line without cutting your hand, yet as soon as the spike is removed the hitch disappears. However, do note that the pull can only be in one direction. If the line pulls straight through the hitch, you are pulling the wrong way and must release and retie the hitch in the opposite direction. It may seem like a good idea to use this knot for the rungs of a rope ladder, but my advice is not to do so, as it is too unstable to be safe.

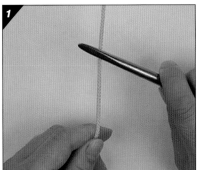

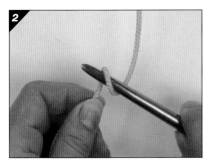

1 Place the spike on top of the line.
2 Make a turn with your left hand round the spike.
3 Bring the tip of the spike back slightly and pick up the line where it goes away.
4 Slide the point of the spike through to catch the far side of the small loop.
5 The hitch is now finished and you will find that you can pull hard in one direction without it slipping. Close up.
6 Finished knot in action.

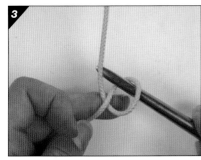

Rolling Hitch

The rolling hitch can be seen as a very sophisticated relation to the clove hitch. It is important to ensure that the second turn locks over the first turn. The rolling hitch is made to pull without slipping in one direction only, with the working part pulling hard down against the two turns, so locking them in place. To pull in the opposite direction requires the knot to be made in the opposite direction. Either version will work satisfactorily with the rope pulling at a right angle.

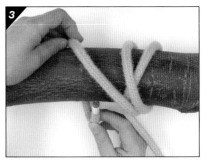

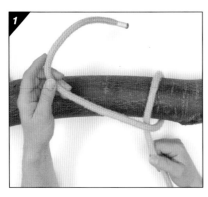

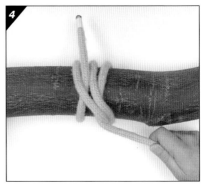

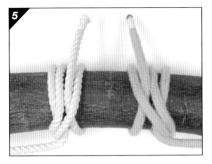

1 Take the working end round a post or spar and trap the standing part.

2 Take another full turn round the post. It should lock in place between the first turn and the standing part.

3 Take another turn round the post, this time passing the other side of the standing part. Tuck it under itself to make a half hitch.

4 The finished rolling hitch note how the pull of the standing part "nips" the first two turns.

5 Finished rolling hitches for pulling in different directions.

6 Finished rolling hitch, right angle pull.

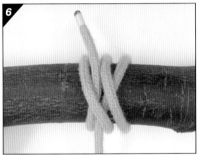

Slipped rolling hitch

By tucking the working end as a bight, a slipped version of the rolling hitch is made. As with all slipped versions of knots, bends, and hitches, care should be taken, but the initial locking turns help to give a good degree of stability to the slipped rolling hitch.

7 The finished knot.

Round Turn and Two Half Hitches

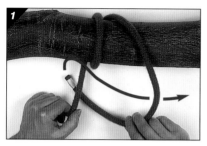

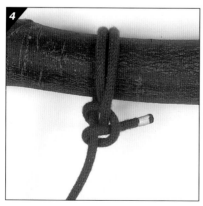

This is an ideal way of making a ship's mooring line fast to a post or ring, the round turn taking a lot of the strain and the two half hitches making all secure. The two half hitches should always be made in the same direction and form a clove hitch round the standing part. Under most conditions and with care the round turn and two half hitches can be released even when there is strain on the standing part of the rope.

1 Take the working end of the rope round the branch two turns making a full round turn.
2 By bringing the working end round behind the standing end and tucking a half hitch is made.
3 Bring the working end round the standing end and tuck to make a second half hitch.
4 Pull tight to finish knot.

Buntline Hitch

Buntlines were ropes attached to the foot of a square sail and were used to spill the wind from the bunt or belly of the sail when the sail was being furled (stowed). This hitch was the hitch used to make the buntlines fast, as it was very secure—the more flapping and tugging the tighter it became.

As the square-sailed ships disappeared, so did the buntline hitch, the only place that it survived was when used to tie a gentleman's necktie, when it was called the four-in-hand knot.

However, the buntline hitch has come out of retirement as it has been found to be an ideal knot for use with the high-tech ropes made of Kevlar.

1 Bring the working end of the rope through the ring and round the standing part.
2 Take the working end round the standing part above the turn it has just made.
3 Tuck the working end through between ring and the turn to make a half hitch trapped in the turn.
4 Pull up snug to produce finished knot.

Fisherman's or Anchor Bend

It is strange that this variation on the round turn and two half hitches should be called a bend rather than a hitch. The way that the first half hitch is passed through the round turns gives a great deal more permanence and bestows upon it the right to be called a bend. This knot is often used to make a rope fast to an anchor or mooring buoy; for added security it is a good idea to seize the working end to the standing part.

1. Take the working end of the rope round the branch two turns, making a full round turn.

2. By bringing the working end round behind the standing end and tucking through the first turns, make what is a trapped half hitch.

3. Take the working end round the standing part and tuck, so making a second half hitch this time outside the round turns.

4. The finished knot.

Cow Hitch

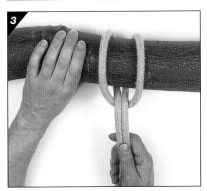

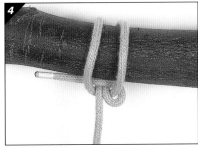

The cow hitch is also called a lark's head. It is a neat way of attaching to a ring or rod a bight of rope or a loop in the end of a rope. This is a good way to fix the eye of a lanyard to a whistle or knife. The pull must always be on both parts of the rope at once; a pull on one side will cause the hitch to slip. If you look closely at this hitch you can see that it consists of a pair of half hitches made in opposite directions to one another. Compare it to the clove hitch where the half hitches are made in the same direction. Do not mix them up.

1   Put a bight of the rope behind the bar.
2   Bring the bight over the bar and pull the pair of strands through the bight.
3   The finished cow hitch, note the pull is to be on both strands.
4   If one strand is tucked behind the bight it becomes the Pedigree cow hitch.

Knute Hitch

A lanyard is a small diameter line attached to a tool, or such like, to ensure that, if it is dropped, it will not go far and can be pulled back to the hand. This is most useful when working aloft, but if you are working at a bench, then the trailing line can get in the way. If the tool has a small hole in it then this hitch, another of Brion Toss's ideas, is perfect for attaching the line as it gives a permanent fixing that can be easily be released. The hole in the tool should only be a little larger than the doubled line, and a figure-of-eight on the working end ensures that it will not pull through by mistake.

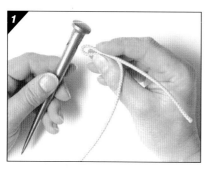

1 Make a bight near the end of the line.
2 Slip the bight through the hole in the tool.
3 Put the short end through the loop formed by the bight.
4 Pull tight and finish the short end with a figure of eight knot for added security.

Highwayman's Hitch

This complex arrangement of loops and bights makes a quick-release hitch. Said to have been used by highwaymen of the past, it works well for all who wish to tether their horses to a ring or rail in a way that enables them to get away quickly. Yachtsmen may find it good for releasing a mooring on a dockside that is out of reach from the boat. Whoever uses this quick-release hitch must be careful that the strain is taken on the correct end of the rope and, as with all slipknots, care must be taken to ensure that the hitch is properly jammed tight so it will not come undone inadvertently.

1   Hold a bight in front of the bar, with the shorter working part on the left side. Bring the working part of the rope behind the bar.
2   Place the working part over the bight. Bring the rest of the working part of the rope, in the form of a bight of rope, round to the front of the bar on the right-hand side.
3   Put the working part bight through the bight in the standing part. Pull tight, first on the working bight, and then on the standing-part bight, to ensure that the hitch is secure. To release, pull the short end.

Timber Hitch

A simple but effective way of tying round a log or bundle of timber—the more you pull the tighter the log is held. If a log is to be dragged along the ground, it helps to put an extra half hitch further along the log, which gives a directional stability to the log as it travels over the ground. The timber hitch is also used at the heart of the diagonal lashing (see page 182).

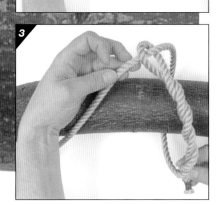

1. Take the working end round the timber, then round the standing part of the rope.
2. Twist the working part round itself by making tucks round with the working end.
3. Continue making up the twist until it is about long enough to go round the timber. Pull on the standing part to tighten the hitch.
4. The finished knot with a half hitch made in the standing part round the timber in the direction that the log will be pulled.

Sheepshank

Over 450 years ago, when the first seamanship books were being compiled, the curious name of the sheepshank ensured that this arrangement of half hitches was guaranteed a mention. From that time on its name and distinctiveness have meant that it is a "must" in all books of knots, even though it is rarely used in earnest. It is best used to shorten a rope without cutting it. To work properly the rope has to have a degree of tension on it. In an emergency, you can also take the strain away from a worn part of the rope by carefully forming a sheepshank around the worn part.

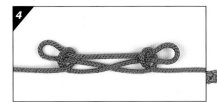

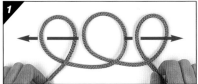

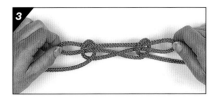

1 Make three half hitches all with their crossings the same.
2 With both hands take the middle hitch and pull through each side hitch, the left hand pulling through from behind the left loop, the right hand making the middle part pass under the left edge of the right hitch.
3 Make sure that the "ears" are well pulled through, and the two side hitches are tight round them.
4 The finished knot.

Two Hearts Beat as One

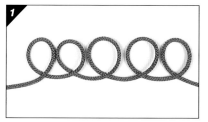

Starting with five half hitches, and then with some careful interlacing and manipulation, a sheepshank variation with two symbolic hearts linked makes a romantic love token.

1. Make five half hitches all with their crossings the same.
2. Overlap the outer two pairs. The right hitch of each pair is moved to the left and over the left hitch, making two "hearts."
3. The center hitch is interwoven through the two "hearts."
4. The finished knot.

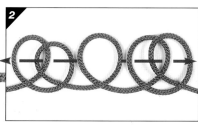

Trucker's Hitch

Trucker's hitch, waggoner's hitch, harvester's hitch, lorry driver's hitch, a dolly: the variety of names given to this method of tightening rope over a load shows that it has been around for a very long time, more often passed on as a trade secret rather than through written sources. Great tension can be applied by using this arrangement of loops and half hitches, yet it can be easily shaken out of the rope when the tension is released. As with all quick release knots, care must be taken to ensure that, as the strain is put on, the loops are big enough not to slip out. There are a number of variations or extra features that help to ensure a greater degree of stability, and it must be realized that the great friction that occurs when strain is applied can wear the rope out if the hitch is always made in exactly the same place.

1   Put a little tension on the part of the rope that is to be tightened. Take the slack part of the rope and make a bight, and place on top of the part of the rope that will be under tension.

2   Form a crossing turn round the bight in a similar manner to the bowline method # 2 (see page 162).

3   Below the first turn, make a second turn round the bight, thus making a little "ear."

4   Keeping a little tension on all parts of the hitch, pull down the lower loop locking the two turns round the "ear."

5   Put a couple of twists in the lower loop.

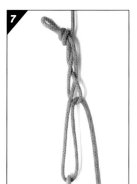

6 Pull a bight of the slack rope through the lower loop.

7 By putting the bight just formed over a hook or cleat and pulling on what was the slack end, great tension can be created.

8 Two half hitches made round the body of the hitch will hold all in place

Jury Mast Knot

A jury mast is a temporary makeshift mast erected to replace a mast that has been lost or damaged.

By a clever interweaving of the half hitches and a careful pulling of loops, four points are made from which to attach the shrouds (those ropes that support the mast). While it is hoped that this knot will never be needed for its proper purpose, it may be enjoyed for its intricacy and beauty.

1 Make three hitches, each with the same crossing, laying the left hitch over the center hitch, and the left hitch under the center hitch.

2 Overlap the outer hitches in the middle of the center hitch.

3 By interweaving your fingers take hold of the overlapped hitches in the center and pull out to make side bights. Notice how the bight to the right will go under and over, while the bight to the left goes over and under.

4 Pull the top of the middle hitch out to make a top bight.

5 The finished knot.

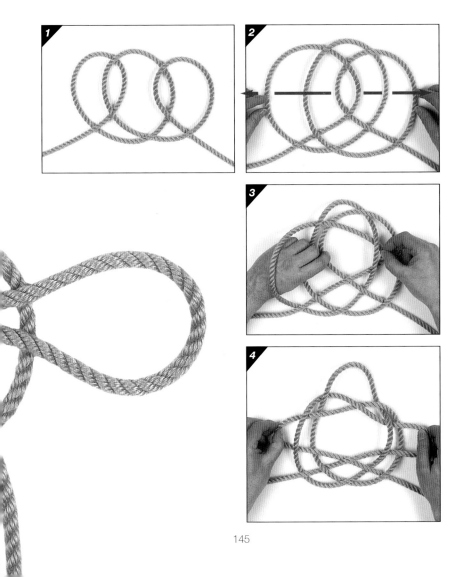

Handcuff Knot

Quickly made, the handcuff knot is a slick bit of knot tying. The trick is to have the rope arranged properly over your hands and to catch the loops with your fingers. If you have need to use this in place of more conventional handcuffs, tighten round wrists and tie off the ends with a reef knot. Escapologists will not bless your knotting skills.

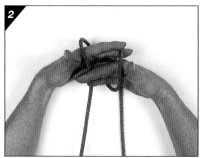

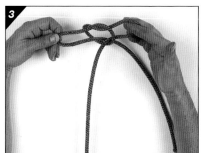

1 Pick up the line in the middle, have the left-hand standing part to the front of your left hand and the right-hand standing part to the back of the right hand.
2 With your left fingers catch the line at the back of your right hand while the right fingers catch the line in the front of the left hand.
3 Pull your hands apart, still holding the line with your fingers.
4 The finished knot.

Fireman's Chair Knot

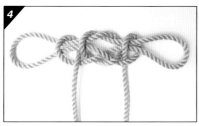

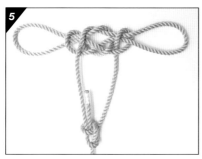

This was used in the past by the fire service to lower people from a building, one loop fitting under the arms the other under the legs. Made mainly without resort to the rope ends, this is quick way of making a pair of adjustable loops that may then be locked into place. The short end must be tied off as a bowline before any strain is put on the chair knot.

1 Make two half hitches with the same crossing, as if you were to be making a clove hitch method # 1 (see page 104).
2 Pull the inner part of the left hitch under and up through the right hitch, while at the same time pulling the inner part of the right hitch over and down the left hitch, giving two "ears."
3 Lock the end by making a half hitch to the right.
4 Lock the other side by making a half hitch to the left.
5 Finish off by tying the short end to the long end as in a bowline.

Prusik Knot

In 1931 Dr. Carl Prusik came up with this method of making a series of loops that would slide up and down a heavier climbing rope, yet lock when strain is put on the loop. Loosen the sling slightly and it can be moved up or down again as required.

For this to work properly, attention to detail is important. The sling should be made from rope at least half the size of the main rope. The ends of the sling should be tied neatly, perhaps with a double fisherman's knot which should never be in the turns round the main rope. In wet, icy, or slippery conditions an extra couple of turns could be made round the main rope. Check that it holds properly before using it in earnest.

To the climber the term "to prusik" has come to mean to use a number of sliding/locking loops to ascend or descend a heavier rope using the Prusik knot or one of its many variations.

1 Lay a fixed loop or strop of smaller diameter rope over the main rope.
2 Bring the right-hand part of the loop round the main rope and through the part of the loop formed to the left.

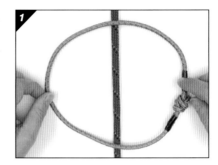

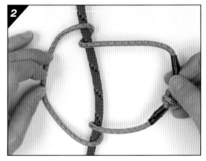

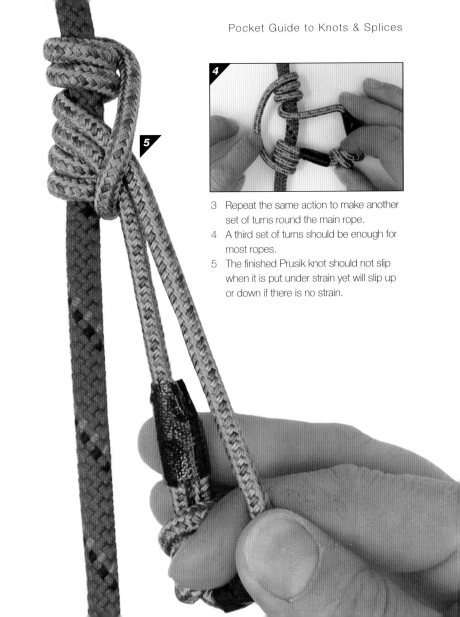

3   Repeat the same action to make another
    set of turns round the main rope.
4   A third set of turns should be enough for
    most ropes.
5   The finished Prusik knot should not slip
    when it is put under strain yet will slip up
    or down if there is no strain.

Bachman's Knot

Bachman's knot works somewhat like the Prusik. It works well on wet or icy rope, with the screwgate karabiner incorporated in the knot enabling it to be released more easily. Note that the strain can only be taken in one direction and when tension is released there can be a tendency for the whole arrangement to slip down the rope. The rope that forms the sling should be no more than half the diameter of the main rope. Whatever you do, do not hang from the karabiner, it is only to be used to ease the knot before moving.

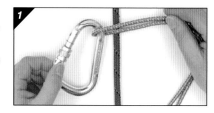

1 Put a loop or strop of smaller diameter rope in a karabiner and lay it by the main rope.
2 Bring the loop of rope round the main rope and through the karabiner.
3 Repeat the wrapping round the main rope and karabiner.
4 After one or two more wrappings the knot is finished and should not slip when strain is put on the loop. The karabiner is used to ease the knot—IT MUST NEVER TAKE ANY STRAIN.

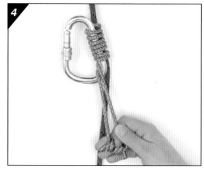

Klemheist Knot

Another variation on the Prusik knot that works well with a loop or sling of soft tubular tape as well as thin rope. The top loop should be very short to ensure a good grip. The turns must lay neat, snug, and, as always, test before using. Tension should only be put in the one direction.

1 Lay a loop or strop of rope or tape across the main rope.
2 Wrap round and round up the main rope until there is a small loop left at the top.
3 Bring the main part of the strop up through the small top loop.
4 By pulling down the main part of the strop, the knot will grip round the rope. For the knot to work successfully, it is important to start with a small top loop.

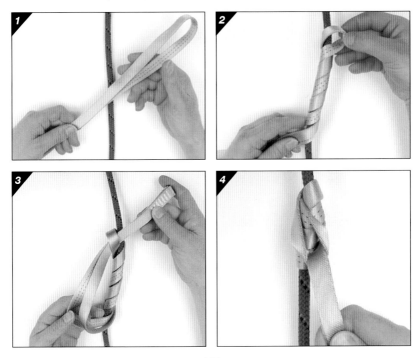

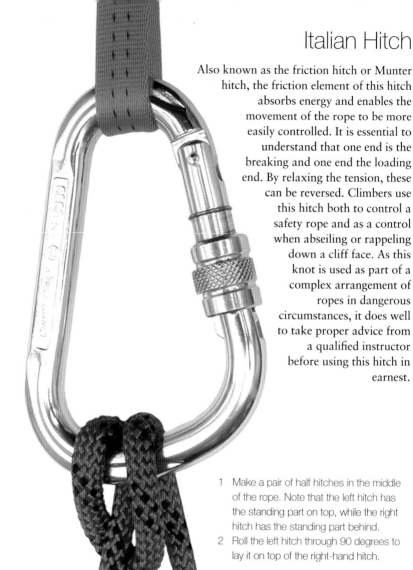

Italian Hitch

Also known as the friction hitch or Munter hitch, the friction element of this hitch absorbs energy and enables the movement of the rope to be more easily controlled. It is essential to understand that one end is the breaking and one end the loading end. By relaxing the tension, these can be reversed. Climbers use this hitch both to control a safety rope and as a control when abseiling or rappeling down a cliff face. As this knot is used as part of a complex arrangement of ropes in dangerous circumstances, it does well to take proper advice from a qualified instructor before using this hitch in earnest.

1 Make a pair of half hitches in the middle of the rope. Note that the left hitch has the standing part on top, while the right hitch has the standing part behind.
2 Roll the left hitch through 90 degrees to lay it on top of the right-hand hitch.

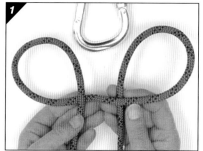

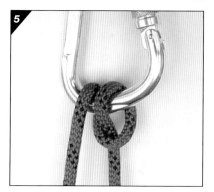

3 Put the pair of loops into the karabiner.
4 The rope on the left is taking the load, the right rope is the brake.
5 By relaxing all strain on the left rope and pulling the right rope the hitch can be reversed to act in the reverse manner— the left rope now being the brake and the right rope taking the load.

Palomar Knot

Quick and simple to tie, the Palomar knot is a strong and secure way of attaching any type of fishing line, even the most slippery of monofilament nylon, to a fishing hook with an eye. Wet the knot with a little saliva after it is tied to help it pull up neat and snug.

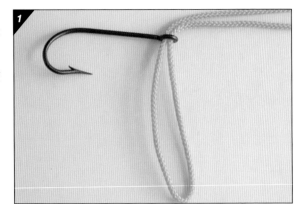

1 Near the end of the fishing line pull a bight of the line through the eye of the hook.

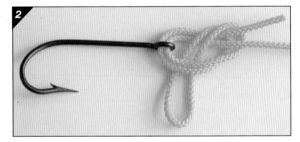

2 Take the bight under the standing two parts of the line, round and down through the loop making an overhand knot.

3 Bring the bight over the end of the hook.

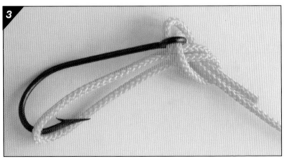

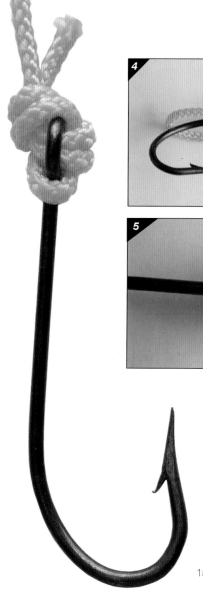

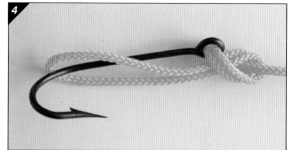

4   Allow the bight to slide back toward the eye as you gently pull on the main part of the line. The bight should slide to become small and tight up against the eye of the hook.

5   Trim off the short tail (practice line may need a little coaxing and nylon a little lubrication). The finished knot in practice line.

Snelling a Hook

Originally fishing hooks were made with a flattened or spade end rather than an eye, and some still are. This method of attaching the fishing line to the hook will work for either. There are lots of turns round the body of the hook and it helps, if using monofilament nylon, to moisten the knot with a little saliva to help these turns to slide up tightly.

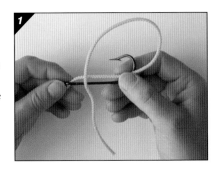

1 Bring the line through the eye of the hook if there is one and lay along the shank of the hook. Bring the short end round to form a loop with the end on top.
2 Bring the short end out parallel with the shank of the hook.
3 Bring the loop round the shank of the hook and pass it over the end of the hook.
4 Carry on bringing the loop round.
5 As the loop is worked round the shank of the hook ensure that it passes over the short tail which should be held in place.
6 Continue to pass the loop round and round over the end of the hook and the short end.

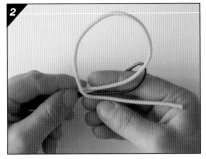

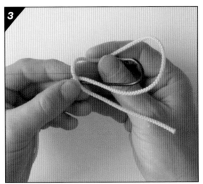

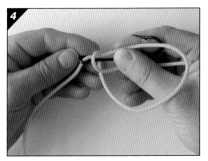

7 When enough turns have been made, pull on the main part of the fishing line to tighten securely round the shank of the hook.

8 Finished knot in practice line (practice line may need a little coaxing and nylon a little lubrication).

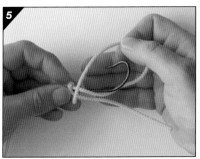

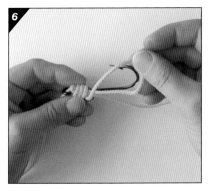

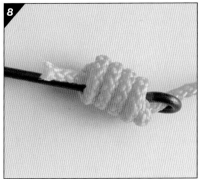

Half Blood Knot

Also called the clinch knot, this is a simple method of tying fishing line to a swivel or a hook with an eye. As with all nylon monofilament fishing line, the turns of this knot will bed down best if lubricated with a little moisture.

1 Put the end of the line through the eye of the hook.
2 Twist the short end round the main part of the line three or four times.
3 Tuck the end of the line back through the start of the twist.
4 Finally, pull tight (practice line may need a little coaxing and nylon a little lubrication).
5 Finished knot in practice line.

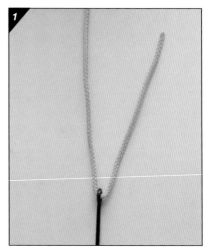

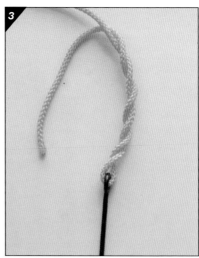

Loop Knots

Loops can be knotted at the end of the rope or in the middle. They may go round your waist or over an object or through a ring. They may be fixed or they may slide: make sure you use the correct one.

Index of Loop Knots

Bowline

Nobody knows where this near perfect knot came from. It is named after the rope attached to the leech (the fore edge of a sail) of a square sail. The rope is tensioned to make the sail stand closer to the wind.

If you study the finished bowline you will notice that the knot has the same form as the sheet bend. Called by many the "king of knots," its only disadvantage is that it is difficult to undo when under strain. Without a load on the standing end it is simple to untie, even after a great strain has been applied.

There are a number of ways of tying the bowline, two of which need to be learned to make full use of this loop knot. The first is best if the rope is coming from behind you—for example, if you need to make fast to the towing point on a car or if you are on a boat and need to put the bowline over a post.

The second method is with the standing end running away from you—useful for when you have had a rope thrown to you or if you want to make the loop round your waist. By learning both methods, you should be able to cope with all eventualities. Whichever method you use, always leave the working end long enough so that it does not pull out as the knot tightens.

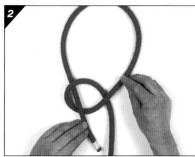

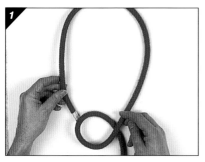

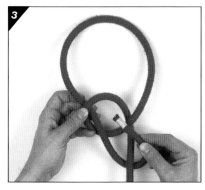

Method #1

1. A little way back from the working end make a crossing turn with the working part on top. Go on to form the size of loop you require.
2. Bring the working end up through the crossing turn—it will go under first, then lie on top of the other part of the turn.
3. Bring the working end round behind the standing part and down through the crossing. Boy Scouts will remember being taught that, "the rabbit comes out of the hole, round the tree and back down the hole again."
4. Finished bowline.

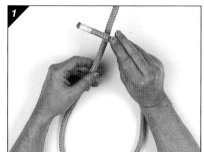

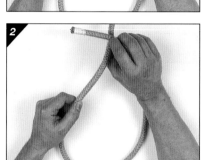

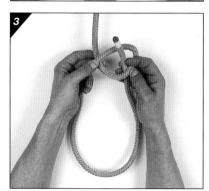

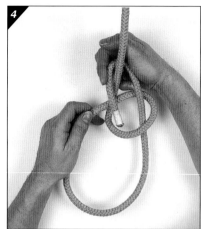

Method #2

1   With the standing part of the rope away from you, take the working end in your right hand and place it on top of the standing part.
2   Put your thumb under the standing part.
3   Twist your right hand 180 degrees away from you, to form a crossing turn with the working end sticking up and through.
4   Take the working end round behind the standing part.
5   Bring the working end down through the hole formed by the crossing turn, and pull tight to finish the knot.

Round turn Bowline

By making a double turn at the beginning of the bowline there is an added degree of security for very slippery ropes

6   The finished knot.

Stopped Bowline

To make certain that the short end will never pull through or work loose, it may be tied off with an overhand knot round the arm of the loop.

7   The finished knot.

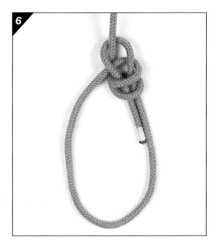

Bowline on a Bight

The bowline on a bight is a neat and clever way of making a pair of loops in the middle of a piece of rope (the bight) without having to tuck the ends. If the strain is not being taken equally by both of the standing ends, then it is sensible to tie off the short standing end with a half hitch or overhand knot.

1 With the rope double form a crossing turn and bring the bight out of the center of the crossing turn as the start of a bowline method #2 (see pages 164–65).
2 Take the bight that has come up through the crossing and enlarge it so it will go over the double rope loop.
3 Lift up the double rope loop and bring the bight of the rope behind the loops and crossing turn—it should be behind the standing part pair of ropes. Tighten the bight round the standing parts.
4 The finished knot.

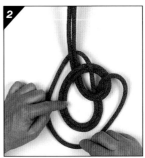

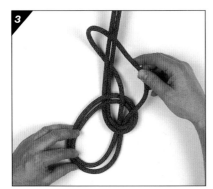

Figure-of-Eight Loop

The figure-of-eight loop, also know as the Flemish loop or double figure eight, is much favored by climbers. The figure-of-eight loop can simply be made in the bight of the rope, but if there is the need for the loop to go round an item or through a ring, then the threading or doubling method needs to be adopted. Climbers feel that, whichever method is used, the distinct shape and ease of tying means that this loop knot is the least likely to be tied incorrectly. The distinctive shape helps when the knot is checked. In fact, if tied incorrectly it becomes an overhand knot which, while not ideal, is not a complete disaster. For best performance from the figure-of-eight loop, always make sure that the pair of lines lie neat and flat within the knot.

Method #1

1 With the rope doubled, bring the bight round and over itself before going under the standing parts.
2 Put the bight down through the loop you have created to complete a figure-of-eight knot tied in doubled rope.
3 Work tight and even to finish the knot.

Method #2

1. Tie a figure-of-eight knot loosely in the rope, leaving enough rope to make the loop and to double the knot.

2. Tuck the working end back on itself following the path round behind the standing part.

3. Bring the working end down through the figure-of-eight to continue doubling the original knot.

4. Bring up and out of the figure-of-eight knot, which is now completely doubled.

5. The finished knot.

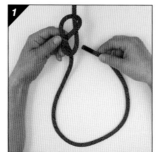

Single Bowline in the Bight

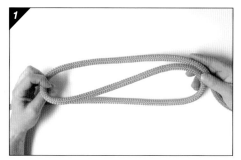

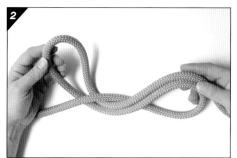

In many ways this loop is both a variation on the bowline and a variation on the figure-of-eight loop. The strain can only be taken in one direction, but it is very useful if you have a very long rope and you wish to apply strain along its length.

1 Pull out a bight and fold it away from the final direction of pull.
2 Bring the bight over then under the part of rope that is to be pulled, leaving a loop with one side doubled.
3 Put the bight down through the loop.
4 The final knot.

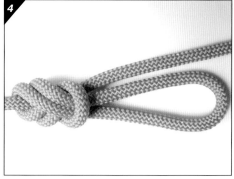

Alpine Butterfly Knot

Sometimes called the lineman's loop, this knot can be tied quickly in the middle of a climbing rope, and is ideal for an attachment point for a third climber to clip on between two other climbers. The strain can be taken in any of three directions, up or down the rope or directly out from the rope.

1 Wrap the rope round your hand giving three turns across your palm.
2 Take the left turn and move it to the right between the other two turns.
3 Take what is now the left turn and bring it over the right two turns, it should then pass behind those two turns to form the loop.

4   With the thumb and forefinger of your left
    hand, pull the loop out from behind the
    two turns.

5   Tighten to complete the Alpine butterfly
    knot.

Angler's Loop Knot

As its name suggests, this is a useful knot for anglers to use to make a loop in the end of their line.

However, it has an even more useful purpose, as Geoffrey Budworth pointed out. It works very well to make a secure loop in that most difficult of materials—shock or bungy cord, an elastic cord that has many uses but in which most knots just keep on slipping. When you are using this knot in bungy cord, do make sure that the working end is long and that you give working end, standing end, and the actual loop a good tug to ensure that the knot is very snug and tight.

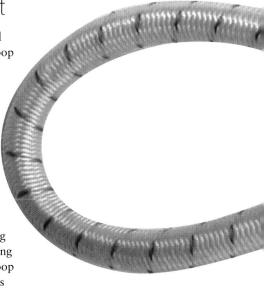

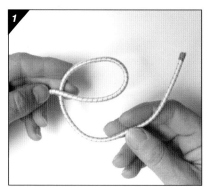

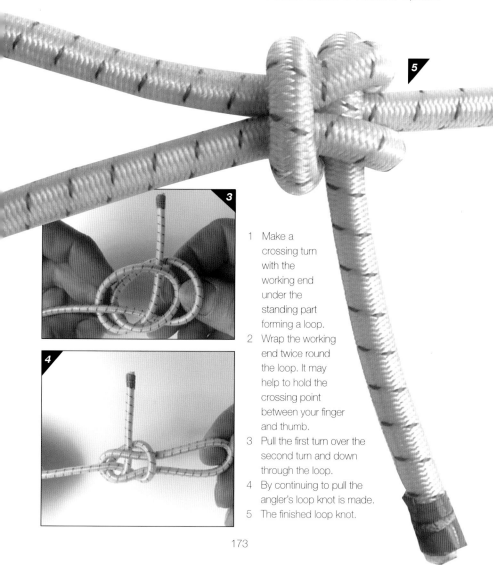

1 Make a crossing turn with the working end under the standing part forming a loop.
2 Wrap the working end twice round the loop. It may help to hold the crossing point between your finger and thumb.
3 Pull the first turn over the second turn and down through the loop.
4 By continuing to pull the angler's loop knot is made.
5 The finished loop knot.

Overhand Loop Knot

An overhand knot tied in the bight gives a very simple loop of no great use. However, a loop made in the same way with a double overhand knot makes a good loop in monofilament nylon fishing line. It also looks pretty good when an ornamental loop is required, but do not expect to be able to untie it.

1 Fold the rope back on itself to make a bight and then make a crossing turn with the working end (the bight) underneath.
2 Bring the bight down through the center of the crossing turn and pull tight.
3 This makes the overhand loop knot.

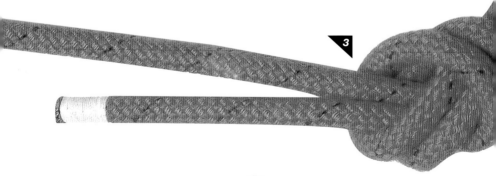

Double Overhand Loop Knot

1   After starting the overhand loop knot, but before pulling tight . . .
2   . . . tuck the bight a second time down through the middle of the crossing turn.
3   Pull tight, working the turns neat.

Englishman's Loop Knot

This is sometimes called the fisherman's loop knot as it works in the same way as the fisherman's knot (see page 116) with the two overhand knots pulling snugly against one another. This pulling together is heavily symbolic, and this is one of a number of knots called the "true lover's knot." Pulling the overhand knots one way will give the oneness of true love, pull the other way and one after another the overhand knots can be slipped undone . . . how sad!

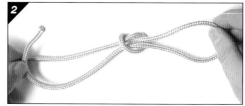

1 Make a crossing turn and tuck the bight down through the center.
2 With the short working end, tie an overhand knot round the standing part.
3 The two overhand knots apart.
4 The two overhand knots pulled together—the finished knot and symbol of true love.

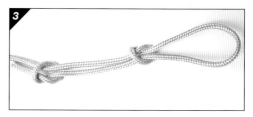

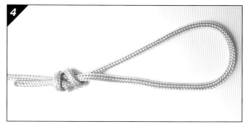

Double or Triple Overhand Noose

Made in much the same way as the Capuchin knot (see page 42), this sliding loop or noose grips tightly round an object. Tied each end of a light line, it is ideal for fixing a lanyard fast to the arms of sunglasses or reading spectacles so they can hang round the neck when not in use. By carefully pulling on the short working end, you will be able to ease the grip sufficiently to enable the lanyard to be removed.

The same system but with more of the initial turns works well as an attachment to fishing swivels.

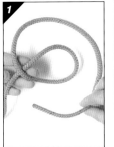

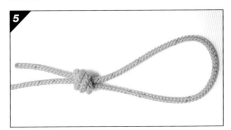

1   Make a crossing turn with a fairly long working end on top.
2   With your fingers parallel with the standing part, wrap round the standing part two or three round turns.
3   Put the working end down through the "tunnel" where your fingers have been.
4   Tighten the turns by pulling on the working end, working the turns snugly together.
5   The finished knot.

Lashings

Lashings are used to join together poles, spars, or other pieces of wood They are often used in combination with each other to build or repair structures.

Index of Lashing Knots

Square Lashing

A square lashing ties two poles or spars together at or very close to 90 degrees. The rope used to make the lashing should be considerably smaller than the size of the poles. For the lashing to be effective, each turn must be pulled as tight as possible as it is made. Some people will even hammer each turn with a mallet to gain maximum tension. The final set

of turns, called frapping turns, are added to pull the main turns even tighter on to the poles. The clove hitch used to start the lashing is best positioned so that it will take any downward strain, and the finishing clove hitch put on the other pole.

1 With the vertical pole on top of the horizontal pole, make a clove hitch on the vertical pole just below the horizontal pole.
2 Bring all the rope round behind the horizontal pole.
3 Bring the rope over the vertical pole and back behind the horizontal pole back to the clove hitch. Pull tight.
4 Carry on making two or three more complete turns right round the two poles, pulling tight after each turn.

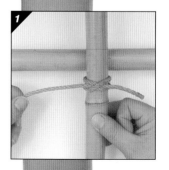

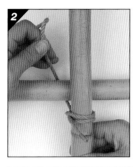

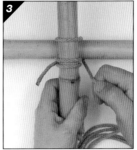

5 After passing the clove hitch, bring the rope round the horizontal pole from behind and start to wrap round the junction between the two poles. These are the frapping turns—pull them as tight as possible.

6 Make two complete sets of frapping turns.

7 Finish off with a clove hitch round the horizontal pole.

8 The finished lashing.

Diagonal Lashing

This is the lashing to be used at a crossing point, where perhaps the poles have a tendency to spring apart. The whole lashing starts with a timber hitch round both poles, pulling them together. When making the main turns, pull each as tightly as possible, then finish off with a couple of frapping turns to tighten even further. Finish off with a clove hitch on whichever spar is the most convenient.

1 Make a timber hitch round the two crossed poles.
2 Take a turn round the two crossed poles pulling the timber hitch tight.
3 Make two or three more complete turns in the same direction, pulling as tight as possible.
4 Change direction by coming round just one of the poles.
5 Make three or four full turns round the two poles at right angles to the original turns, again pulling as tight as possible.
6 Take the working end of the rope round one of the poles so that you can make frapping turns.
7 Make two complete lots of frapping turns.
8 Finish off with a clove hitch.
9 The finished diagonal lashing.

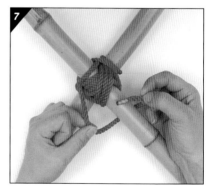

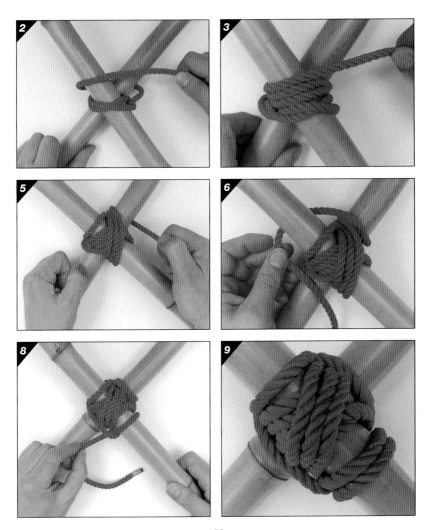

Sheer Lashing

Sometimes called a round lashing, the sheer lashing has two distinct uses. First, it creates an "A" frame or set of sheer legs using a single sheer lashing. Second, two or three sheer lashings can be used to bind together a couple of poles to make a longer spar. To make the "A" frame, two poles are put side by side, the lashing made at one end. Start with a clove hitch round one of the poles. Next, put on the initial turns, but do not pull them very tight. When it comes to the frapping turns, they, too, are not pulled very tight, for when the lashing is finished the "legs" are opened to make the "A" and this tightens everything up.

A slightly different approach is needed to join two poles together to make a longer pole. Overlap the poles a good distance and start with either a clove hitch, a constrictor knot, or a timber hitch round both poles at one end of the overlap. Follow by a series of turns, each of which must be heaved as tightly as possible, for this time there will be no frapping turns to tighten the lashing further as there is no space between the poles. Finish your lashing with a clove hitch round both poles, tucking the end down inside the lashing if possible. Make a second lashing at the other end of the overlap. Occasionally it is necessary to made a third lashing in the middle.

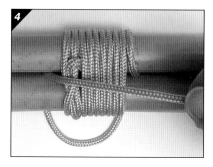

1. Start by making a clove hitch round both poles.
2. Wrap round both poles, trapping the end of the clove hitch.
3. Carry on making eight to ten more turns round the pair of poles. The lashing could now be finished with a clove hitch round both poles or . . .
4. . . . put in a couple of frapping turns by bringing the end of the rope between the two poles.
5. Finish off with a clove hitch round one of the poles.
6. The finished sheer lashing with the poles parallel.
7. The finished sheer lashing with the poles opened to create a pair of sheer legs or "A" frame.

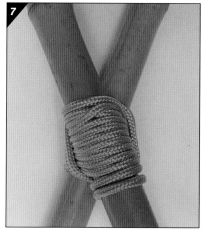

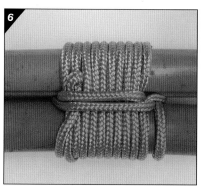

Figure-of-Eight Lashing

The figure-of-eight lashing is used to join three poles together to create a tripod. The three poles are laid side by side and a clove hitch is made round one of the outside poles, a little in from the end. The lashing line is then woven in and out of the poles in, as it were, a figure-of-eight movement. After a series of these passes have been made, frapping turns are put in, the end of the line made off with another clove hitch round an outside pole. The legs of the tripod are now ready to be opened up.

1 Start with a clove hitch round one of the poles, and lead the rope under and over the other two poles.
2 Go round the pole furthest away from the start and weave the rope back over and under.
3 Continue to weave the rope in the figure-of-eight manner for seven or eight full passes before bringing the rope up between two of the poles.

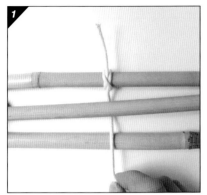

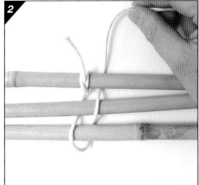

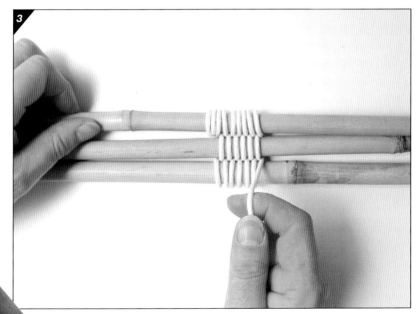

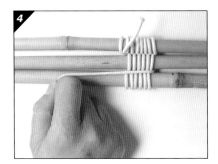

4 Pull the rope parallel to the poles and start to put in some frapping turns.

5 After making frapping turns between the first two poles move on to make frapping turns round the other pair of poles.

6 Finish off with a clove hitch round the pole from which you first started.

7 The tripod can now be opened out.

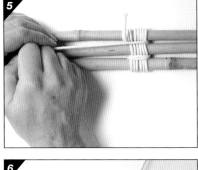

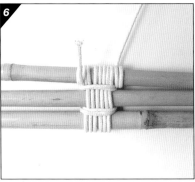

Spanish Windlass

The Spanish windlass is a crude but fairly effective way of tightening a rope using two poles or, for small line, a spike or similar and a bar. Take care, as a surprising degree of tension can soon be built up; you can even get a bit of a "kick back," but it is a useful technique to have in emergencies. It does not do a lot of good to the rope—it tends to distort the lay of the rope and give a great deal of localized friction.

1 With a vertical and a horizontal pole, use the horizontal pole to catch the rope and then twist with the horizontal pole braced against the vertical pole.
2 Bring the horizontal pole square with the vertical and rotate round the vertical pole, passing over/under the rope when it is met.

3 Continue until sufficient tension has been created. Keep the tension by holding the horizontal pole against the rope with your hand or get someone to put on a temporary seizing round pole and rope. **Beware of any kick back.**

Plaits & Braids

Plait is one way of describing it, braid is another, and the old-time sailor would have talked of a sennit—all of these words describe the combination of a number of pieces of line to make a bigger piece, often with a special shape and pattern.

Index of Plaits and Braids

Three-Strand Flat Plait/Braid

The three-strand flat or ordinary plait is the simplest of all plaits and is seen all over the world. This is the hair plait of little girls' pigtails. While often used for decoration, the plait has many practical uses. Plaited in straw or palm leaf, it may be made up into a hat or mat. As the plaiting together of three strands will give a stronger line than the three strands on their own, sailors in the past made up great quantities of plait—or, as they would call it, sennit—from the yarns of worn-out rope, and used it for all sorts of purposes around the ship. It is a simple step forward to make this plait with three pairs of strands or even three times three.

1 Arrange the three strands flat and side by side.
2 Take the outer right-hand strand and bring it over one strand and to the middle of the other two strands.
3 Take the outer left-hand strand and bring it to the middle of the other two strands.
4 Take the outer right-hand strand and bring it to the middle. Continue left to middle, right to middle until the required length of braid is made.
5 A finished length of three-strand flat braid.

Four, Five, and Six-Strand Flat Plait/Braid

It is possible to make a flat plait with four, five, or six single strands using a similar method to the three-strand flat plait. The secret of a good looking plait is that the tension put on the strands used is always the same to give an even effect. You will notice that, as you plait the long ends hanging below your hands, they will get tangled; try and free them as you go. For a long plait it may help to bundle each strand up and hold it in a rubber band or make a couple of half hitches round the bundle. You can release more line as you need it.

Four-strand flat plait/braid

1 Arrange the four strands flat with a space to the middle.

2 Bring right outer strand to the inside over its neighbor.

3 Bring left outer strand to the inside over its two neighbors.

4 Bring right outer strand to the inside over its neighbor.

5 Bring left outer strand to the inside over its two neighbors. Repeat right, left, until required length reached.

6 The finished plait/braid.

Five-strand flat plait/braid

7 Arrange flat with three strands to the right and two to the left. Bring outer right to middle, then outer left to middle.

8 Repeat outer right to middle, outer left to middle until required length made.

Six-strand flat plait/braid

9 Arrange three strands to the right and three strands to the left. Bring outer right to middle, then outer left to middle.

10 Repeat outer right to middle, outer left to middle until required length made.

Four-Strand Square Sennit

With four strands it is possible to plait, braid, or make a sennit that is not flat but square in section. If the same sennit is rolled between the palms of the hand or underfoot, you could also contend that it was round. By making the same sennit with four pairs of strands, it becomes rounder still and is the base from which the so-called "square plait rope" is constructed (see page 17).

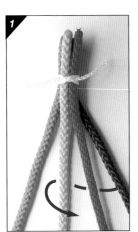

1   Arrange the four strands in a square bundle; open them out slightly with the top two inside the back two, all with a slight space between.
2   Take the outer right-hand strand behind two strands and over to the middle of those two.
3   Take the outer left-hand strand behind two strands and over to the middle of those two.
4   Take the outer right-hand strand behind two strands and over to the middle of those two.
5   Take the outer left-hand strand behind two strands and over to the middle of those two.
6   Carry on right outer, left outer until the required length is made.
7   The finished sennit.

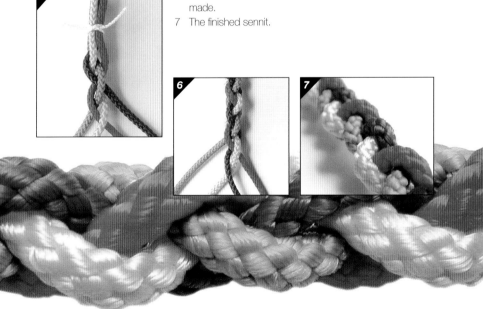

Crown Sennits

The crown knot made with four strands in a similar way to page 54 tied on top of itself repeatedly makes a very great range of interesting and useful sennits. If the crown knots with four strands are each made in the same direction then a round sennit is created. When each crown is made in the reverse direction to the previous crown, then a square sennit is formed.

While it is possible to make a crown sennit with just three strands, it does not work very well. However, if it is made with three pairs of strands pulled good and tight and worked always in the same direction, then a handsome sennit is formed. Four pairs of strands can be worked in the same manner.

Continued on page 200.

Four-strand round crown sennit

1   Make a four-strand crown knot with the strands pointing in a counterclockwise direction. Pull tight.
2   Make another crown in the same direction on top of the first crown. Pull it tight to sit neatly on the previous crown.
3   Repeat until the required length of sennit is made.

It is also possible to make a different sennit using six strands, crowning alternate strands, three strands then the other three strands on top, always in the same direction. Again the same can be done with eight strands, alternating four and four. If you make a plain crown knot using six strands you will notice that there will be a space in the middle. Six strands will not pull up tightly enough to lose the space. If another strand is placed in the middle as a center core, a crown sennit of six strands and a core is made. This form of the crown sennit is useful for covering all sorts of cores, the more strands the bigger the core needed. The use to which you put this whole range of crown sennits is up to your imagination. They can be included in ships' bellropes, rope fenders, the handles of dog leads, key fobs—the list is endless.

Four-strand square crown sennit

1   Make a four-strand crown knot with the strands pointing in a counterclockwise direction. Pull tight.
    Make another crown in the opposite (clockwise) direction on top of the first crown. The strands will point back in the direction in which they have just come. Pull it tight to sit neatly on the previous crown.

2   Repeat this crowning, first in one direction then in another, until the required length is made.

Doubled crown sennits

1 Make the crown with pairs of strands.

2 Repeat crowning with pairs either—as in this example—in the same direction as the previous crown to make a round sennit, or in the opposite direction to make a square sennit.

Three + Three alternate crown sennit

1. With six strands spread out neatly, make a crown knot using every other strand.
2. Now crown the other three strands, making the crown in the same direction.
3. Pull the crown tight so it beds neatly down.
4. Carry on the alternate crowns until the required length is reached.

Six-strand crown sennit

1 Make a crown knot with six strands. Pull as tight as possible—but there will always be a slight hole in the middle.
2 Repeat the crown—in the same direction if a round sennit is required and in the alternate direction if a hexagonal sennit is wanted. If you want, a core can be put in the middle to fill the hole that forms in the center of the sennit.
3 Repeat until the required length is made.

Splices

A splice can be looked upon as a multi-strand knot used to create a permanent join or finish to a rope. A well-made splice is stronger than almost any knot.

Splicing hints

It will help if you tape the ends of the strands, and a Swedish fid will help ensure that the strand follows the right path. The splices shown here use three-strand rope, but the principles apply in the same way to four-strand rope, should you ever come across it. Take trouble to ensure that all the strands of the rope are taking the same amount of strain and everything is good, neat, and fair. Do not trim the ends of the strands too short, as when strain is first applied, they may pop out.

Index of Splices

Back Splice and Tapering a Splice

The back splice forms a permanent finish to the end of a three-strand rope. It makes for a good grip to the end of a piece of rope, but has the disadvantage that the rope is increased in diameter, so may make it difficult to reeve through eyebolts, blocks, and other small holes. The splice starts with a crown knot and then all strands are tucked against the lay in an over one and under one fashion. Treat all strands the same; make one tuck with each of the strands before making the next round of tucks.

Any splice may be given a good, tapered finish. There is a quick taper, often used by sailmakers where first one whole strand is dropped, and the other two strands tucked in the normal way, and then another strand dropped and just one strand is tucked in the normal way. This will give a finished splice with the tails sticking out side by side down the rope rather than round the rope. The splice may be improved by rolling underfoot when all the tucks are finished.

1 Having opened out the three strands neatly, make a crown knot (see page 54). Arrange it so it is good and square on the end of your rope.
2 Take any one of the strands and following a path against the lay (in other words, point the strand in an S direction) and go over one strand and under the next strand.

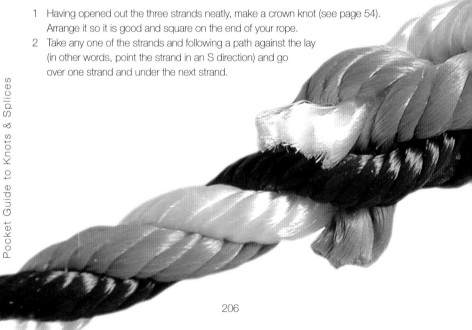

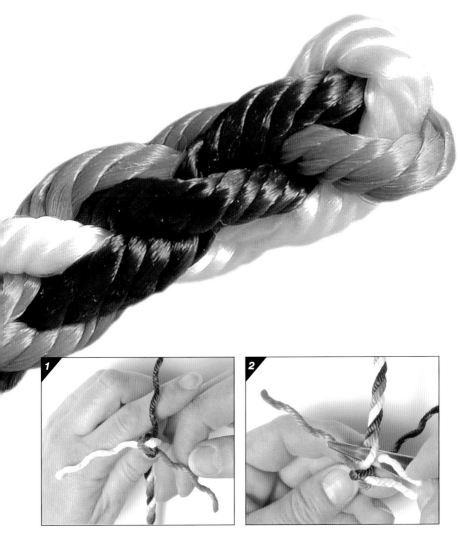

3 Work the strand into a neat position by pulling tight, but not so tight as to distort the rope.

4 Move round the crown to the next strand and tuck this over one and under one strand.

5 Move to the last of the three strands and tuck that over one and under one strand.

6 This completes the first series of tucks. The strands should all come out from under a separate strand and should all be on the same level.

7 Make another series of tucks starting with any strand going over one and under one strand.

8 Complete a full second series of tucks; again, the strands should all come out from under a separate strand and should all be on the same level.

9 Three complete sets of tucks should be sufficient.

10 Trim the end but not too close.

11 Quick taper by dropping one strand and tucking the other two, then tucking just one strand.

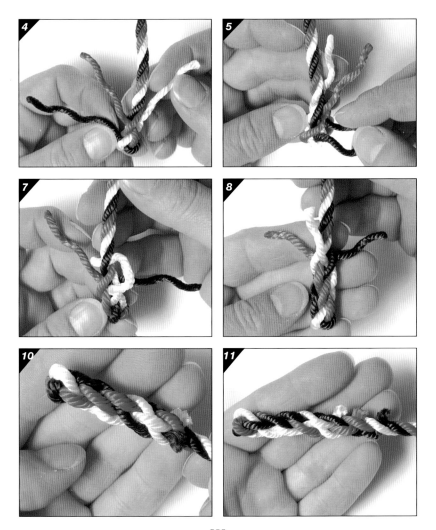

Eye Splice

This is a strong, permanent method of making a fixed loop on the end of a piece of three-strand rope. The first round of tucks can be a little confusing. The unlaid strands should sit neatly against the main part of the rope. Remember to treat each strand equally, tucking under one strand against the lay in turn moving from left to right round the rope.

When one set of tucks is done, the ends of the strands should all be on a level. It may well help to apply a temporary seizing, perhaps a constrictor knot (see page 107), to stop the strands unlaying further back than you want, but remove it when you have made the first set of tucks. Pull up gently to a snug even fit. You want the strain to be taken equally by each of the three tucked strands. Then carry on making further sets of tucks.

For all-synthetic rope make five full sets of tucks; with natural fiber three full sets of tucks is enough.

The eye splice can also be made with a thimble—metal or nylon—in the eye. This gives protection against chafe and also spreads the load out equally down both legs of the eye. It takes a little experience to ensure that the thimble is good and tight after the tucks are put in and the seizing removed. Try to avoid either a space at the bottom of the thimble or a

length of loose-laid rope where the first tucks are made. An eye splice with a thimble is said to be a hard eye, while without a thimble it is called a soft eye.

Whichever type of eye splice, it is best that it is finished off by tapering. This can be best done by cutting out some of the yarns in each of the strands, perhaps reducing the strand

Continued on page 212.

1 Tie a constrictor knot round the rope back from the end of the rope. Unlay the strands back to this point and position the rope so that there is one "leg" either side of the rope and one along the center.

2 Tucking against the lay, tuck the first strand under the strand it is nearest to on the standing part of the rope—in other words, tuck strand # 1 under # 1 in the standing part.

3 Turn the splice slightly and tuck the strand that is to the right of the first strand under the strand that is to the right of the first strand on the standing part of the rope. In other words tuck # 2 under # 2 on the standing part.

4 Now turn the splice more and tuck # 3 strand under # 3 in the standing part. This tuck should also be against the lay.

by a third and make a complete round of tucks, then reducing the strand by half to complete the final round of tucks.

The splice may be improved by rolling underfoot when all the tucks are finished.

5   The strands should now all stick out on the same level.

6   Tuck the strand over one and under one just as in the back splice for two more complete sets of tucks if a natural fiber and four more sets of tucks if a synthetic fiber rope. The ends can then be trimmed—but not too short.

7   The ends may be tapered by dropping one third of the yarns in each strand and tucking; then dropping half of those left and tucking.

8   A finished hard eye splice.

Short Splice

This splice joins together in a very strong and permanent fashion two ends of rope of the same size. The bringing together of the two sets of strands so that they fit snugly together is called marrying the rope.

To start with, a temporary seizing can be of help, especially with some of the nylon and polyester ropes that have a tendency to unlay very easily and quickly. Remove the seizings when the first set of tucks both ways have been made. Make the tucks in sets—first one side, then the other, until five full sets of tucks in each direction have been made. Three full sets of tucks would be enough if the rope were made from a natural fiber.

The best splices are tapered to a finish. A well-made short splice is very strong but it does increase the thickness of the rope.

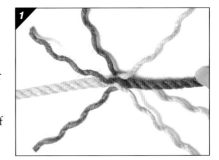

1   Unlay both pieces of rope and interlace the strands so that they alternate one from each side of the splice. This is called marrying the rope.
2   A temporary seizing, perhaps a constrictor knot, will help to keep the two ropes together for the first series of tucks.
3   Take one strand on one side and tuck against the lay over the strand next to it and then under the next strand.

4 Tuck the second and third strand in a similar manner so that one side of the splice has a complete series of tucks.

5 Turn the rope round. With the other three strands tuck over one and under one strand.

6 When a set of tucks has been made in each direction the seizing can be removed, and any slight slackness in the splice tightened up by a gentle tug on each strand.

7 Make two more complete sets of tucks on each side (if natural; four more if synthetic). Trim the ends to finish and roll underfoot to round the splice.

8 The finished splice.

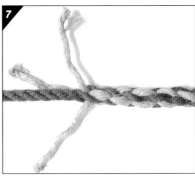

Long Splice

As the short splice makes the rope fat, it may prevent it running through a block or passing through an eye. The solution is to make a long splice, where the action is spread out in three places, so reducing any increase of diameter to a minimum. Some versions of the splice leave the rope at almost exactly the same diameter, making the join almost invisible. There are so many versions and opinions as to how this can be achieved, all of them with their own merit, giving credence to the saying, "different ships different long splices." The version shown here is a basic version, good for general working. It must be noted that whatever long splice is made, it will not be as strong as a short splice

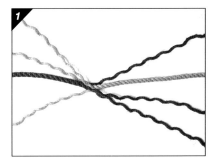

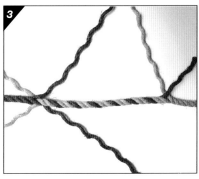

1 Unlay plenty of rope on both strands and "marry" the ends by interlacing the strands so that they alternate, one from each side of the splice.
2 Decide on a pair of strands, one from each piece of rope. Gently unlay one strand and carefully lay the other in its place.
3 This should bring one pair of strands a long way from the middle or marrying point.

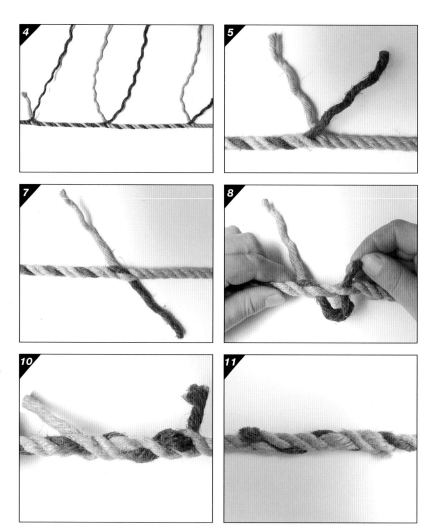

4 Leave one pair of strands in the middle, and with the other pair lay and unlay until there are three separate pairs of strands.

5 Trim the longest strand of the pair down to a workable length.

6 Make the first part of a reef knot by tucking the left strand over the right strand and then under.

7 Pull the knot tight. It should bed down neatly or you have tucked in the wrong direction.

8 Bring one of the ends over itself and under the adjacent strand tucking against the lay of the rope.

9 Repeat with the other strand.

10 Make a second tuck over and under with both strands.

11 This completes one of the three sets of strands; now repeat with the other two sets of strands.

12 With the ends of the strands tucked and trimmed at each of the three places the long splice is complete.

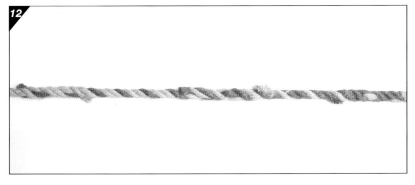

Right-Angle Splice

This is a useful splice to be used where one rope needs to join at right angles to another rope the same size or even a little bigger. For example, if you are making up a rope ladder, a scramble, bowsprit, or other heavy net.

1   Unlay the strands of the rope that will be used to join the main rope. Spread the strands flat. Tuck the left-hand strand against the lay of the rope under two of the strands in the main rope.

2   Tuck the middle strand under one strand. It will come out of the same exit point as the first strand.

3   Tuck the third strand under two strands, this time going in at the same point as the middle strand went in.

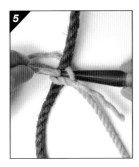

4 Tuck the left strand down over two strands of the main rope and under the middle strand of the joining rope. Tucking against the lay of the rope.

5 Tuck the right-hand strand over two strands in the main rope, then underneath itself.

6 Turn the ropes over and tuck what was the middle strand over two strands in the main rope and under the last strand that as yet has not had a strand tucked under it.

7 The strands should now all come out at the same level. Pull up any slack.

8 Tuck all strands over one and under one in the normal splicing manner. After one more set of tucks (three more sets for synthetic rope) the splice can be trimmed and finished.

9 The finished splice.

Decorative and Fancy Knots

Turk's heads are nothing more than a continuous plait of a single piece of line round something. When finished, they appear to have no beginning or end. They are found all over the world in many sizes and complexities, tied in a range of materials and even carved in stone. Their uses are as varied as the materials they are tied in; sometimes as functional but decorative bindings, sometimes as an item on their own. The initial knot is made as a single-ply woven band; it may then be followed round a second or third time to double or triple the knot. To help describe Turk's heads we count the number of loops—called bights—on the edge of the ring, and the number of strands that go to make up the kind of plait before it is doubled or tripled—we call them leads or parts. As you create the knot, look out for the formation of "diamonds" and "ladders"—these will be needed later as the knot evolves. It is best to make the simpler Turk's heads round your hand, then transfer it to where it is wanted. It can be tightened round the object.

Index of Decorative and Fancy Knots

Three-Lead, Four-Bight Turk's Head

This is one of the simplest of the Turk's heads to make. It is a ring of three-strand plait without a start or finish, with four bights on the edge of the ring. Once the initial knot has been made, it can be followed round to double or triple it. As well as being a round ring this simple Turk's head can also be flattened into a small mat with a beautiful design. A three-lead, four-bight Turk's head, doubled and flattened as below, is the symbol of the International Guild of Knot Tyers.

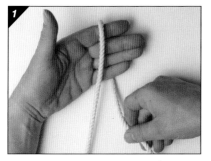

1 Lay the rope over your hand with the standing part at the front of your hand. The working part should be long enough to go loosely round your hand at least three or four times.

2 Bring the working part up and over the standing part.

3 Take the working part round the back of the hand and up to the left of the standing part.

4 Bring the working part over to the middle of the two turns.

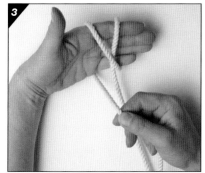

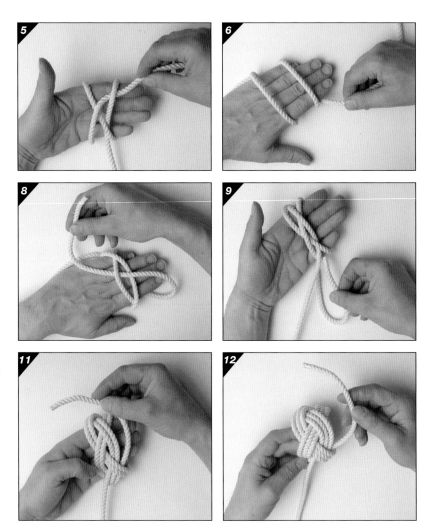

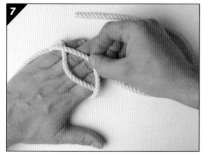

5 Tuck the working end under the right-hand turn. This is the beginning of the continuous flat braid.

6 Turn your hand over to show the two turns at the back.

7 Bring the left turn over the right turn, to make a "diamond." This will also make a little more of the braid.

8 Tuck the working end to the left under what is now the left turn.

9 Turn your hand back; the working end should mate with the standing part completing three turns that form a continuous braid of three leads and four bights.

10 Tuck the working end to start the doubling process.

11 The Turk's head can be doubled, if you run out of the working end complete by going the other way with the standing part. If you are making the knot to fit round an object you will need to work the slack out of the knot with a spike.

12 A further following round will treble the knot.

13 The finished knot from the end showing the four bights.

Three-Lead, Five-Bight Turk's Head

A very slightly different start will give rise to a three-lead, five-bight Turk's head. Tied in the same material, this will make a ring with a little larger diameter. This Turk's head can also be flattened to make a small mat.

1 Bring the working part round the hand and over the standing part.
2 Bring the working part round behind the hand and up to the right of the standing part and over the strand that is to the right.
3 Tuck the working part under and then bring it over to the left.

4 Turn your hand over.
5 Bring the right turn under the left turn to make a "diamond."
6 Tuck the working part up through the gap and over to the right.

7 Tuck to the left under the right turn. Note that this clearly creates the braid design we are making.

8 Turn the hand back and tuck following the line of the standing part. The Turk's head is now ready for doubling or trebling.

9 The finished knot doubled.

Four-Lead, Three-Bight Turk's Head

The start of this Turk's head is the constrictor knot (see page 107). Open the constrictor knot out a little and with one of the working ends complete the under/over/under weave and you will have a slightly wider (four-lead) but small diameter (three-bight) Turk's head ready for doubling or trebling.

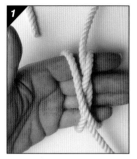

1   Make a constrictor knot.
2   Having brought the working end round behind the hand, open out a "diamond" with a bar across, from the under pair of strands.
3   Lead the working end under, over, under, diagonally through the "diamond." This may be thought of as following a "diamond ladder."
4   Bring the working end round behind the hand and up, following the line of the standing part, to commence doubling the knot.
5   The complete knot doubled.
6   The complete knot trebled.

Four-Lead, Five-Bight Turk's Head

The more leads and bights, the more complex the start. As you make the passes round your hand, look out for the way that paths or ladders are prepared for the future when you will need to pass under, over, under, over to lock the structure into its continuous weave. If you find difficulty with keeping passes in place, you may prefer to try making this knot round a rolled piece of cardboard and hold the line in place with pins. Use this Turk's head when you want a wider band with a larger diameter. When you are familiar with making the four-lead, five-bight Turk's head, use it to cover a "T" junction such as the place where a spoke on a ship's wheel touches the rim or the handle on a corkscrew. Because of the even number of leads, it is possible to split the leads each side of the junction.

1 Bring the rope round the hand and tuck under itself, open out the "diamond."
2 Bring the rope round the hand and passing under the standing part and up through the "diamond." This will create a "diamond ladder" for later.
3 Tuck by going over then under to the left. This will form a "diamond ladder." Keep it in place, it will be used in the next cycle of passes.

4   Pass behind the hand, over the standing part and then follow under, over, under, diagonally across the first "diamond ladder."

5   Now tuck to the left over, under, over diagonally across the second "diamond ladder."

6   Bring the working end round behind the hand and follow the standing part back into the Turk's head to start doubling the knot.

7   The finished knot doubled.

8   The finished knot covering a T junction.

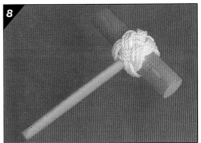

Five-Lead, Four-Bight Turk's Head

By starting in the same way as the beginning of the three-lead five-bight Turk's head, this knot goes on to grow into a longer Turk's head of five leads and four bights.

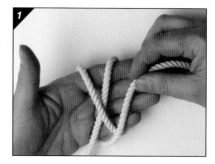

1. Take the rope round the hand, over itself, and round the hand again, passing the standing part to the right and over—this is stage two of the three-lead, five-bight Turk's head. Then tuck under, over to the left.

2. Bring round behind the hand and tuck under, over following the line of the standing part.

3. Turn the hand; the working part goes over, then tucks under and over.

4. Bringing the working part on round the hand and turn the hand back. The working end should be to the right of the standing part. Tuck over, under, over along the "ladder."

5. Turn the hand again and tuck under, over, under, over.

6. Turn the hand back; the working end can now follow the standing part to double the knot.

7. The completed five-lead, four-bight Turk's head.

True Lover's Knot

Knots can be symbols and in this true lover's knot the two overhand knots are linked, symbolizing love joining separate halves to make one, but each part still free to move. This knot can be found made up into rings and bracelets. To enable the knot to sit properly, notice that each of the overhand knots is the mirror of the other.

1. Make an overhand knot (see page 38) in one strand of the rope.
2. Bring the other rope up through the overhand knot, round under itself, then over and down, making a second inter-linked overhand knot.
3. The finished knot with other true lover's knot pieces of jewelry.

Sailor's Cross

The true lover's knot made in a single piece of rope can, with a simple couple of pulls, become a cross. The same technique is used to decorate pairs of cord in China and Japan, where the knot is a symbol of good fortune and complete virtue.

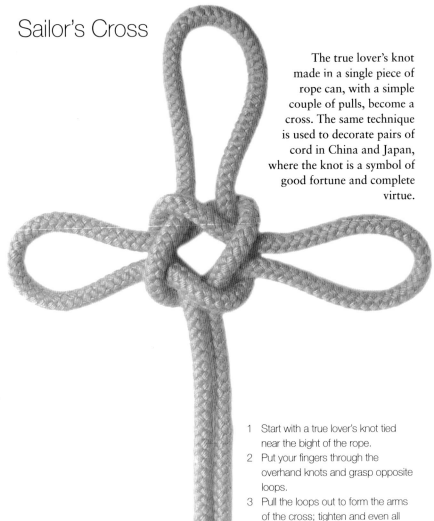

1   Start with a true lover's knot tied near the bight of the rope.
2   Put your fingers through the overhand knots and grasp opposite loops.
3   Pull the loops out to form the arms of the cross; tighten and even all points of the cross.
4   The finished sailor's cross.

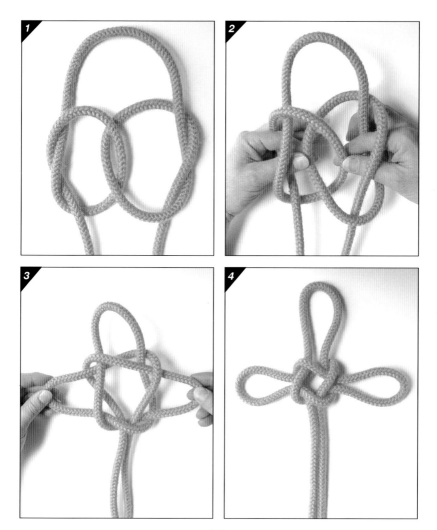

239

Bosun's Whistle Lanyard Knot

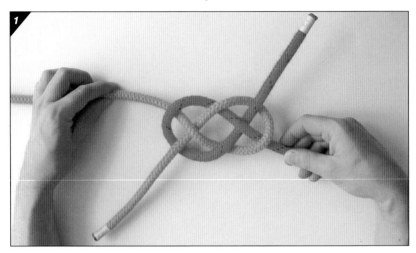

This knot is known by many names, including bosun's whistle lanyard knot, marlinespike lanyard knot, sailor's knife lanyard knot, two-strand diamond knot, single-strand diamond knot, or just plain lanyard knot. Whichever name you adopt, you will have a beautiful knot tied with two strands of rope. Notice that the start is a carrick bend with the working ends diagonally opposite each other.

1 Make a carrick bend (see page 114) with the working ends coming out on top on opposite corners of the knot.

2 Take the right-hand working end round in a counterclockwise direction going over the left standing part and then up through the middle of the carrick bend.

3 Take the left-hand working end round in a counterclockwise direction going over the right standing part and then up through the middle of the carrick bend.

4 Pull tight to complete the knot—you may have to work the slack out of the knot with a spike.

Doubled Bosun's Whistle Lanyard Knot

Before tucking the two ends up through the middle of the Bosun's whistle lanyard knot, it is easy to double the knot using the two working ends. Having made this knot you can go on and make other knots or you can trim the working ends tight at the knot to make a button knot.

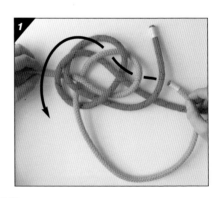

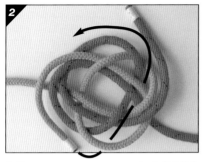

1. Start with a single Bosun's whistle lanyard knot (see page 240), tied loosely. It will be doubled by following each of the standing parts into the knot.
2. One at a time follow in from each standing part, each to go about half way round the original knot.
3. Before completing the cycle of the original knot, form the knot loosely into shape and then put the working ends up through the center of the knot. The working ends should pass round and pull in the standing parts.
4. Pull tight and work out the slack.
5. The finished knot.

Ocean Mat

Just as Turk's heads capture some knot tyers' imaginations, so do flat knots or mats. The ocean mat, sometimes called the ocean plait mat, is a good mat to start with. From the simple overhand knot a couple of pulls, twists and tucks will give a handsome design. You may find it helps to pin the design out as you go. It is possible to extend this design by further pulls, twists, and tucks. Once the initial design has been made it may be followed round two, three, or more times to make the finished mat.

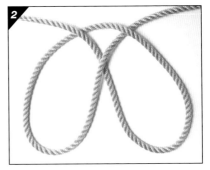

1 Start with an overhand knot (see page 38).
2 Pull down two bights to form "ears," leaving the two ends sticking up and out of the knot.
3 Twist the "ears" in a clockwise direction.

4 Keeping the twist in the "ear," move the right "ear" over the top of the left "ear."

5 Weave the right-hand end down, over, under, under, over, and out at the opposite corner of the mat.

6 The reason for going under two in the middle with the first end is to provide a complete under, over, under, over, under path for the second strand to follow. This locks the whole interweave pattern in place.

7 One of the ends can now start to double the mat.

8 The finished mat doubled. It could, of course, also be trebled or even followed round four or five times if enough material is available. It will require careful working into an even shape.

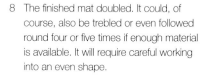

Prolong Mat

Start in the middle of the rope with a carrick bend with the working ends on the same side, loops can be pulled out, twisted and ends tucked in the same way as the ocean mat was made. The prolong mat has one more bight or loop on its side than the ocean mat, and it may also be extended or "prolonged" in the same way.

1 Start with a carrick bend (see page 114) with the working ends on the same side.
2 Pull out bights to form "ears."
3 Twist the "ears" in a clockwise direction.

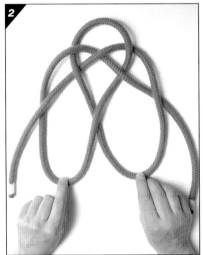

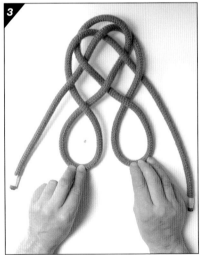

4   Pull the right hand "ear" over the left.

5   Take the left-hand working end under, over, over, under, and out.

6   Weave the right-hand working end over, under, over, under, over, and then round to start to double the mat.

7   The finished mat.

Danish Kringle Mat

Made up from a series of interlinked components that have the form of the
overhand knot, this mat was so named by Kai Lund after the sign that hangs
outside the pastry shops in Denmark. A coaster-sized mat can be made with
about three to four yards of eighth of an inch diameter cord. A small doormat
would need about 30 yards of half-inch diameter rope.

1 Create the first element of the mat by almost making an overhand knot, but not actually tucking the end through.

2 Make a second element; this time the line will lock the lower diagonal in place.

3 Continue to make and lock elements until four have been formed. The fifth element will interweave with the first to complete the mat.

4 The whole mat consists of five elements, all interlinked. It can now be doubled.

5 Doubling the mat.

6 The mat doubled; it can be trebled or even quadrupled.

Half Hitching

A very simple series of interlocked half hitches makes a very effective decorative covering for almost anything from knife handle, flagon, needle case, water bottle, to rope fenders. The hitching may be worked in very fine material with a needle, or in large rope for the largest of tug fenders using a large spike or fid. One thing to be remembered about half hitching is that it takes a long time. Many people who start covering an object with half hitching think that they must be doing it incorrectly as it takes so long. As a guide, you are doing very well if you can hitch eight to ten yards in an hour. There are lots of variations on the basic "stitch" that will give a differing texture and effect. Probably the most useful is the use of one or two lazy strands. These strands do not actually do any work, but they do help the work grow a lot quicker.

Continued on page 252.

1 To start, take a turn of rope round the object to be covered and make a half hitch round the turn
2 Continue to make more half hitches round the turn.

The lazy strand can be of a different color to the main working material and this will add a further interest to the finished work. Half hitching can cover almost any shape by the adding or decreasing of the number of hitches used, giving a technique that knows no bounds except your imagination.

3 Keep on making half hitches going right round the object, until you arrive at the first half hitch you made, then make a half hitch through the bottom of that very first hitch.

4 Continue to make half hitches through the bottom of the previous row of hitches. This continues until the object is covered.

5 If the object gets bigger, you may increase the number of hitches by making a double pair of hitches rather than just a single hitch. If the object tapers (decreases in size), just skip one hitch.

6 Carry on hitching as usual after any increase or decrease.

7 For quicker coverage a lazy strand may be put in place and the half hitch made round it as well as the previous row of hitches.

8 A ship's bow fender being covered with half hitches.

Glossary

Belay To tie off, to make fast. To attach one climber to another or to a fixed point with a rope that will absorb the shock of a fall.

Bight The rope folded back on itself to form a narrow loop.

Bollard A short wood or metal post on a boat, ship or Quat used for securing a mooring rope.

Cable A large rope made by twisting together three small ropes of three strands.

Chafe Wear caused by abrasion.

Coil Rope made up in neat series of circles usually for storage purposes.

Cordage A general term to cover all sorts and sizes of rope.

Crossing Turn A circle of rope made with the rope crossing over itself.

Eye The hole inside a circle of rope; a permanent loop made at the end of a rope. The ring at the end of a fishing hook.

Fid A pointed wooden tool used to separate strands of rope when splicing, also used to round out eyes, grommets, etc.

Frapping Turns Additional turns made in lashings, whippings, and seizings to tighten the main turns.

Grommet A continuous circle of rope.

Half Hitch A crossing turn, often made round an object. The crossing holds the lower part in place.

Halyard A rope used to raise and lower sails on a ship.

Hard-Laid Rope Any rope that has been constructed with a tight twist or braid and is therefore stiff to handle.

Heaving Line A light line with a weighted end, thrown from boat, either to rescue someone in the water or to then pull a heavier rope.

Holdfast A fitting or fixed object to which a rope under strain can be attached.

Karabiner An oval or D shaped metal snap link usually with a screw-lock used by climbers.

Laid Rope Rope made by twisting.

Lay The direction of the twist in the rope

Line Another word for rope but generally small cordage of less than half an inch in diameter.

Marlinespike A slim pointed metal tool used to separate the strands of rope, and splice wire rope, helpful to untie knots.

Make Fast To tie up or secure a rope to something.

Pricker A tool rather like a marlinespike but having a wooden handle.

Palm A glove-like leather strap fitted with a metal plate. This is worn on the hand and used to push heavy needles through rope or canvas.

Rigger One who works on the rigging of ships.

Rigging The ropes both fixed and moving on a ship.

Seize To join two ropes or parts of ropes together with a binding of small cordage.

Sheath The woven cover of a braided rope.

Sheet A rope that controls the sails of a ship.

Shock Cord A rope with a core of rubber and a braided nylon sheath. This gives a high degree of stretch, also known as elasticated cord or bungy cord.

Sling A continuous circle of rope or tape either premade or made by joining the ends of a short piece of rope with a fisherman's knot or water knot.

Small Stuff A general term to cover any type of small cordage.

Spar A wood or metal pole.

Spike A general term for any pointed rope working tool, be it an awl, fid, marlinespike, pricker or Swedish fid.

Standing Part That part of the rope not immediately being used in the tying of a knot.

Standing Rigging The rigging of a ship that does not move.

Strand One of the larger parts of a rope.

Strop Another word for sling.

Swedish Fid A tool with a hollow, pointed end and wood handle, useful for splicing rope and working decorative knots tight. So called, as this tool was first patented in Sweden in 1949.

Tape A flat woven webbing sometimes of a tubular construction, used by climbers to make slings.

Three-Strand Rope A rope made from three strands twisted together.

Tuck To pass one part of a rope under another.

Turn The passing of a rope around one side of an object.

Twine Small softly twisted cordage of less than an eighth of an inch in diameter.

Unlay The act of untwisting or taking apart the strands of a rope.

Whipping A permanent finish to the end of a piece of rope made with very fine twine.

Working End The end of the rope used during the tying of the knot.

Yarn Natural or synthetic fibers twisted together as thread.

Bibliography

Asher, Dr Harry: *The Alternative Knot Book*; Adlard Coles.

Ashey, Clifford.W.: *The Ashley Book of Knots*; Doubleday, New York; Faber & Faber, London.

Biddlecombe, George: *The Art of Rigging*; Dover reprint, 1848.

Grainger, Stuart: *Creative Ropecraft*; Adlard Coles.

International Guild of Knot Tyers: *Knotting Matters*, and other publications; 1982 and to date.

Lever, Darcy: *The Young Sea Officer's Sheet Anchor*; Dover Reprint, original dated 1808.

Smith, Phil: *Knots for Mountaineering*; California, 1953.

Toss, Brion: *The Complete Rigger's Apprentice*; International Marine

Turner, J. and van de Griend, P. (editors): *History and Science of Knots*; World Scientific.

The International Guild of Knot Tyers

Founded in 1982, the guild is a registered charity with the declared object of "the advancement of education by the study of the art, craft and science of knotting, past and present." The Guild regularly publishes a magazine *Knotting Matters* that is sent to all members. There are now well over a thousand members in over twenty-five countries. Groups of members meet together both in small local meetings and much larger international meetings. Membership is open to all who have an interest in knot tying be they highly skilled or just beginners. For more information please contact:

The Honorary Secretary.
Nigel Harding
16 Egles Grove,
Uckfield,
East Sussex
TN22 2BY England.